WICCA

CRYSTAL MAGIC

A BEGINNER'S GUIDE TO CRYSTAL SPELLCRAFT

LISA CHAMBERLAIN

STERLING ETHOS
New York

STERLING ETHOS
New York

An Imprint of Sterling Publishing Co., Inc.

Originally published as *Wicca Crystal Magic* in 2016 by Wicca Shorts

ISBN 978-1-4549-4102-6 (print edition)
ISBN 978-1-4549-4101-9 (e-book)

Distributed in Canada by Sterling Publishing Co., Inc.
c/o Canadian Manda Group, 664 Annette Street
Toronto, Ontario, Canada M6S 2C8
Distributed in the United Kingdom by GMC Distribution Services
Castle Place, 166 High Street, Lewes, East Sussex, England BN7 1XU
Distributed in Australia by NewSouth Books
University of New South Wales, Sydney, NSW 2052, Australia

For information about custom editions, special sales, and premium and corporate
purchases, please contact Sterling Special Sales at 800-805-5489
or specialsales@sterlingpublishing.com.

Manufactured in Canada

2 4 6 8 10 9 7 5 3 1

sterlingpublishing.com

Design by Gina Bonanno and Sharon Leigh Jacobs
Cover by Elizabeth Mihaltse Lindy
Picture credits—see page 113

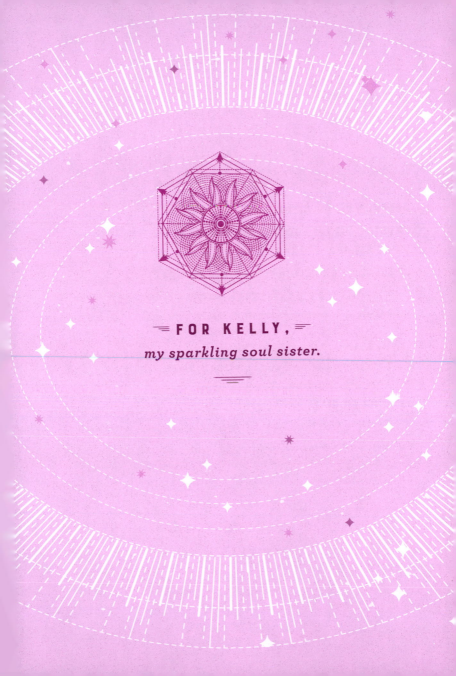

FOR KELLY,

my sparkling soul sister.

CONTENTS

PART THREE

A CRYSTAL GRIMOIRE

INTRODUCTION

SINCE THE TIME OF THEIR FIRST DISCOVERY, PEOPLE HAVE delighted in the beauty of naturally occurring crystals found within the Earth's crust. Ancient cultures in Egypt, Greece, Rome, China, Japan, India, and South and Central America are known to have used crystals in the creation of jewelry, art, weaponry, and even cosmetics. These colorful gems have long held spiritual significance as well, as evidenced by the variety of crystals found at prehistoric gravesites and stone monuments all over the world.

In popular culture, certain crystals like diamonds, emeralds, and rubies have always been revered, serving as symbols of love and affection as well as wealth and success. But the world of crystals is far vaster than these rare stones, with an enormous variety of minerals in all shapes, colors, and sizes. Many crystals and other mineral stones are becoming more accessible to the average person than their famous "cousins" in the gemstone family. Due to their much lower cost, gorgeous stones like amethyst, rose quartz, and jasper can be used in larger quantities for a wealth of purposes. For example, some stones are ideal for promoting a calm, peaceful energy in the home, while others may absorb electromagnetic frequencies (EMFs) from electronic devices, protecting the nervous system from "EMF overload."

Over the past several decades, the popularity of crystals in healing and the magical arts has seen a resurgence. Of course, magic itself has been a big topic of focus since the turn of the twenty-first century, thanks in large part to its role in novels, movies, and television shows (and regardless of whether it's accurately portrayed!). But crystals owe their prominence in modern times to the healers of the New Age movement (see page 9), who embraced many alternative forms of medicine from diverse traditions around the world at a time when remedies outside the realm of mainstream Western medicine were generally considered "quackery." These New Age pioneers revived and revamped crystal healing, which had been relied upon by physicians in former centuries, and it continues to be practiced today.

Crystal healing is not the same as crystal magic, yet it's worth pointing out that healing and magic have not always been separate domains, and natural magical allies like crystals are good reminders of the connection between the two. Healers and magicians both draw from the same energetic properties of the stones, but use different methods for achieving results. Both disciplines utilize the crystal as a means of manifesting an intention. In healing, the intention is generally to resolve an imbalance in the body, usually through placing the crystal on or near the physical body of the one needing assistance.

Balance and good health are not only goals of crystal healing but also goals of magic. The difference is that in magic, the desired result is manifested first on a nonphysical level through focused visualization on the intended outcome, before it arrives in physical form. In other words, the attention is all on the metaphysical realm, rather than the biological reality of the situation. This process is what makes magic so versatile in its applications; any intention you can focus on and believe in has the ability to manifest, from health to wealth to love and joy. Crystals, with their diverse energetic frequencies, can resonate with—and therefore help to bring about—all of these magical goals.

Crystals are unique elements in modern natural magic. They're like herbs in that they're natural and originate in the ground, yet they don't "grow" and can't be planted, cultivated, or even harvested, unless you're one of the few who can dig them out of your backyard. Non-mineral stones, aka "rocks," such as those found on a beach or along a river, can resonate with energy and are used in plenty of magic, but the minerals that form what we call crystals have a more concentrated power when it comes to specific magical purposes. Crystals can create energetic changes on their own. This is due in part, it seems, to the chemical makeup of the individual mineral and its specific energy signature. Something about their origins deep within the Earth also gives crystals a special, mystical, even majestic life force of their own.

This guide provides an overview of the many uses of crystals in magic and the underlying principles of the Universal forces that make it all work. It's written from the perspective of Wiccans and other Witches, but you need not consider yourself a Wiccan or a Witch to benefit from the information here. We'll start by identifying the characteristics that distinguish a crystal or mineral stone from a plain old "rock." We'll then take a look at the relationship between crystal healing and crystal magic and how the two coexisted before they came to evolve separately over time. Some core principles of magic are explained with specific relevance to crystals to show you how their unique energetic vibrations can help you consciously shape the reality of your daily life on the physical, emotional, and spiritual planes.

To work crystal magic, you will need at least one stone, though a good handful of a few different types is ideal. Part two of this guide will introduce you to thirteen of the most popular and accessible crystals and their primary uses as well as instructions on how to care for and charge them. Finally, you will find several spells and magical workings centered around these thirteen stones. There are traditional spells using one or more charged crystals along with other spell ingredients as well as more "hands-on" workings like magical baths, crystal charms, and even magically charged drinking water!

Remember that with any kind of magic, intuition and intention are the driving factors, but experimentation and practice are what lead to success. Be persistent as you work to incorporate your new knowledge and be sure to let the crystals and stones guide you in your process, as they make wonderful guides on the spiritual path. Blessed Be.

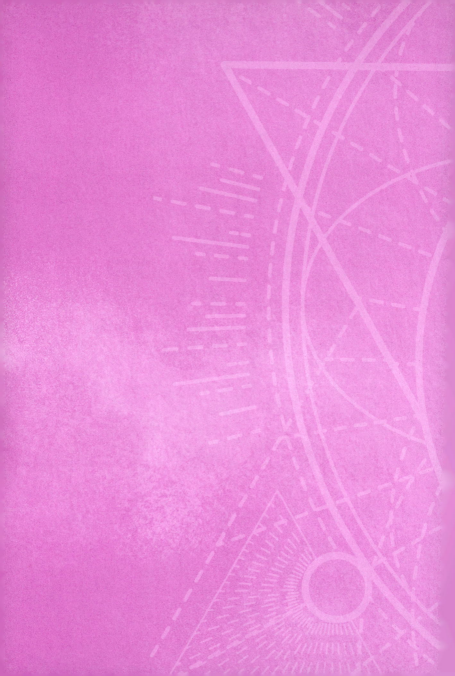

PART ONE

GIFTS FROM THE EARTH

AN ANCIENT RELATIONSHIP

PEOPLE HAVE RECOGNIZED THE MAGICAL POWER OF STONE since before recorded history. As far back as 11,600 years ago, the oldest known stone temple was built at Göbekli Tepe in Turkey. The famous sites of Stonehenge, Newgrange, and other ancient stone monuments around the globe are also testaments to our long history with this most fundamental building block provided by the Earth. Stone's ability to shelter our early ancestors surely had something to do with the importance it held in the spiritual lives of the communities who built these mysterious structures, yet the pillars, carvings, and geometric arrangements of monuments like these point to a deeper connection with stone that went beyond basic survival needs.

Today, many people still build *cairns*, or deliberately stacked vertical columns of stones, in natural areas like coastlines and hiking trails. Cairns may be used as place markers, memorials to the deceased, or tributes to the unseen spirits of the natural world. There is a widespread tradition of making, carrying, and giving away "wishing stones," which are small enough to be carried in pockets and often have words like *love, peace*, and *luck* carved into them. Customs like these seem to point at a collective, if unconscious, desire to commune with the energies of the Earth itself, even within the landscape of our modern lives.

Stones come in all shapes and sizes and can be made of many different natural materials, but there are certain treasures sourced from the Earth that have always held particular power for spiritual seekers, including Wiccans and other Pagans. Generally found inside larger masses of rock under the Earth's surface, crystals and other mineral stones are used in magic for everything from protection to divination to manifesting wealth and love. Like the stone temples, these practices have a long history of their own. Ancient Egyptians, Greeks, and Romans alike used quartz crystals as talismans. Indigenous peoples in the American Southwest have revered the powers of turquoise since the time of the Ancestral Puebloans. To the ancient Chinese, jade represented the moral virtues of human beings and was used to make ritual objects. Indeed, throughout time, in any culture where minerals and crystals were accessible, those who recognized the powers of these stones incorporated them into their daily spiritual lives.

In Wiccan and other modern Pagan traditions, crystals may be used in many facets of spiritual and magical practice. One common use for crystals and stones is to mark the sacred circle before a ritual begins. They are also used to honor deities, with specific stones sacred to particular gods and goddesses. In keeping with centuries of tradition, they are still used in amulets, talismans, and other good-luck charms as well as for scrying and protection. Some magical tools, such as wands and pentacles, are decorated with crystals. These special stones can also be used to protect, purify, and otherwise enhance the energy of any indoor or outdoor space. And of course, crystals and stones can be powerful components of spellwork, which is the main focus of this guide.

Over the following pages, we'll delve into the history of crystal magic, and examine a few core esoteric principles that illuminate why crystals are such excellent magical tools. First, however, we'll cover a bit of terminology to get a clearer picture of what's meant when people talk about "crystals and stones." We will also take a brief look at the relationship between crystal magic and crystal healing, which has existed throughout much of human history and which is largely responsible for the resurgence of crystals in modern magical practice. By the end of part one, you'll have a solid introduction to the world of crystals, and you'll be ready for the magic to begin!

CRYSTAL, STONE, OR ROCK: WHAT'S THE DIFFERENCE?

MANY SOURCES, INCLUDING THIS GUIDE, OFTEN USE THE terms crystal and stone interchangeably. This is because the technical differences between the two in terms of their physical makeup aren't really significant when it comes to magic. The more appropriate term in any case is *mineral*, as it covers crystals as well as most other types of stones used in crystal magic. (There are a couple exceptions, which will be discussed below.) In other words, not all minerals are crystals, but all crystals are minerals. While it's not necessary to understand the technical distinctions between crystals and other minerals to work successful magic with them, it's useful to have a sense of what distinguishes them from rocks.

Minerals are defined as any inorganic substance that is formed naturally through the Earth's underground geological processes, which involve the interaction of heat, pressure, and fluid. Every mineral occurs in a solid state at normal Earth temperatures and has a specific, consistent chemical composition. Of the thousands of known minerals, metals like gold, silver, and copper are perhaps the most commonly recognized, but several others are also of interest to humans. Minerals occur in a very wide variety of shapes and colors and may be found as a standalone specimen or in a mixture with other minerals.

Most of the stones involved in magic and healing are composed of single minerals, such as hematite, malachite, and turquoise. There are some exceptions, however, including lapis lazuli (Latin for "blue stone"), which is a mixture of the minerals lazurite, diopside, and others. There are also a few substances that are often referred to as minerals or stones and are made of organic matter. Jet is fossilized wood, for example, while amber is the fossilized resin of trees.

Crystals are minerals with a specific atomic structure that forms a regular pattern, which creates the points, flat surfaces, and other interesting geometric forms we tend to think of when we hear the word *crystal*. Snowflakes are a good example of something with a crystalline structure and has six arms or sides growing symmetrically from a single droplet of water. Probably the most common type of crystal that people are familiar with is quartz crystal, which is used in watches, clocks, and many other electronic devices. True "crystal balls" are made from the clearest varieties of quartz. Other forms, especially rose quartz and amethyst, are also very common and are useful for a wide variety of magical and healing purposes.

Rocks are solid pieces of the Earth that may contain two or more minerals, along with organic matter such as coal or shale. Unlike crystals and pure minerals, rocks don't have a consistent composition. Usually, the mineral content of a rock comes in the form of microscopic grains rather than large chunks. However, one exception is the *geode*—a hollow rock lined on the inside with crystals. These form when water leaves mineral deposits inside the cavity within the rock, which slowly grow into crystals, often with stunning results. Geodes can contain single or multiple minerals. The most common types are lined with quartz, amethyst, agate, and sometimes combinations of all three.

Depending on the context, the word *stone* can be essentially interchangeable with *rock*, but the latter word tends to bring to mind drabber, less distinctive objects. For example, lapis lazuli, since it's comprised of two minerals, technically qualifies as a rock, but you'll rarely hear it labeled as such. *Stone* is often the preferred term when the item in question is of interest for use by people, such as for building, making art, or working magic. Some Witches will affectionately and jokingly refer to their personal crystals as their "rock collection," but by and large the preference for a catch-all term in this department is *stone*. In the general context of magic, *stone* can refer to a crystal, a mineral, a geode, or even a simple pebble from a bubbling stream.

Finally, some sources will use the term *gemstones* to refer to both crystals and certain other minerals. Meaning "precious stone" or "jewel," this term is not rooted in science or magic but is instead a category of particularly attractive and often rare minerals used in jewelry. Some minerals used in healing and magic, such as garnet and fluorite, are considered gemstones, though there isn't universal agreement on what exactly qualifies as a gem. At any rate, the word *gemstone* was used widely by healers and magical practitioners during the Middle Ages and is used in some sources on Witchcraft and magic today.

CRYSTAL CONNECTIONS: MAGIC AND HEALING

O F THE VARIOUS TOOLS OF MAGIC FOUND WITHIN WICCA, crystals have a unique connection to what we often call the "New Age" movement, which emerged in the late twentieth century. New Agers promoted healing with crystals, meditation, channeling, and other forms of alternative medicine and spirituality. While many Wiccans do not identify as participants of the New Age movement, we do owe something to these spiritual pioneers who brought crystals back out into the light after centuries of disuse. After all, it was the popularity of crystal healing that led to a wider availability of crystals and other mineral stones than at any other time in history.

Alternative healing modalities incorporate crystals and other stones in a variety of ways. Chakra balancing is one major use for crystals, and some practitioners of Reiki, acupuncture, color therapy, and other energy healing techniques incorporate them into their work. Unlike conventional medicine, which focuses on the physical plane alone, crystals work on the physical, emotional, and spiritual planes to effect positive change. Their transformative effects are considered to be more holistic than, say, the effects of an aspirin taken for a headache. Plenty of information has become available about the healing powers of crystals, for physical and spiritual imbalances of all kinds, and while it is still dismissed by many as a pseudoscience, crystal healing has gained more respect in mainstream culture in recent years, with a proliferation of certification programs available online and even in-person in some areas.

Crystal magic and crystal healing are quite different practices in many fundamental ways, but because physical, emotional, and spiritual healing is often a goal of magic, there is quite a bit of overlap between what alternative healers know about crystals and stones and what Witches know. Plenty of alternative healers may also practice magic and vice versa! Raymond Buckland, for example, who founded the tradition of Seax-Wica in the United States, includes gemstone healing in his *Complete Book of Witchcraft*, right in the same chapter as magical poppets.

As we will see shortly, the boundaries between magic and healing were not always as defined as they are today. Many forms of traditional healing often involved elements we would consider magical or even religious, such as chanting, praying, drumming, and other shamanic techniques. Many have argued that the split between the physical and the spiritual when it comes to modern medicine has limited the possibilities for truly effective healing. The resurgence of crystals, which can be used in conjunction with modern remedies, has been part of a movement to remedy this artificial division.

Although the focus of this guide is on the magical aspects of crystal energy, you will also find information about their healing aspects, particularly in the profile descriptions of the thirteen featured crystals in part two. Keep in mind that this information is in no way intended to replace what a trained practitioner in the alternative healing modalities would provide and should never be used in place of medical advice or needed medical treatment of any kind.

A BRIEF HISTORY OF
CRYSTAL MAGIC

COMPARED TO OTHER FORMS OF MAGIC, SUCH AS SPELLWORK involving candles, herbs, incantations, charms, sigils, and the like, crystal magic in its current form is a relatively new phenomenon.

After all, it's only been over the past few decades that the wide variety of crystals we see today has become available on a mass scale. However, Witches and other practitioners of magic have always recognized the powerful energies of stone, whether we are talking about giant rocks, sparkling quartz crystals, or simple pebbles.

Indeed, our relationship with the diverse substances found on and beneath the surface of the Earth goes back to the beginnings of our existence as a species. Rock shelters were among our earliest homes, and stones were being used as tools for as far back as three million years ago. Eventually, humans learned to dig under the surface of the Earth for crystals, metals, and other minerals. Mining has been around for at least 40,000 years, when hematite was extracted and used for pigment in cave paintings.

As for when people began using stones specifically for magical purposes, we can only guess. However, we do know that our early ancestors believed that the natural world is inhabited by spiritual energy—a belief known today as animism. It is reasonable to assume that certain stones and other natural objects were also thought to have what we would now call magical power.

One of the first uses for natural substances that went beyond taking care of basic needs like food and shelter was the making of beads from animal bones, seashells, and stones like jet and amber. Some of these beads date back to at least 75,000 years ago and are believed to have served both as decorative jewelry and as amulets—items worn for protection against negative energy, illness, and other misfortunes. These are likely the first magical items created by prehistoric humans. Many amulets made from Baltic amber have been discovered in Britain, dating back between 10,000 and 30,000 years ago.

Quartz crystal, one of the most abundant minerals on Earth, was clearly valuable to many prehistoric civilizations. Quartz crystals and white quartz stones have been found in gravesites dating back several thousand years in Africa, Asia, the United States, and Europe, suggesting that these stones had spiritual significance to our ancestors all over the world. At Newgrange, the famous megalithic tomb in Ireland that predates the Egyptian pyramids, the outer layer of the entrance wall is covered with pebbles of white quartz. The quartz was brought to the site from an area over 100 kilometers (62 miles) away, which was no small distance in those days and shows how valued this mineral was to the civilization that built the tomb.

Magical Traditions of the Ancient World

While our knowledge of prehistoric uses for crystals and minerals stones is murky, it becomes easier to trace some of today's magical traditions back through time once we get into recorded history. The ancient Egyptians revered several different crystals and mineral stones, including clear quartz, carnelian, emerald, lapis lazuli, malachite, moonstone, tiger's eye, and turquoise. These stones were used in jewelry and protective amulets as well as to promote physical health and psychic receptivity. Stones like lapis lazuli, moonstone, and rose quartz were associated with the goddess Isis. Tiger's eye was often used in statues of deities to represent the eyes of the god or goddess being depicted. In burial rituals, quartz crystals were placed on the forehead of the deceased to guide them on their journey to the afterlife.

In ancient Greece, soldiers rubbed hematite on their bodies before going into battle, as it was believed the powers of this stone would protect them from harm. Sailors wore amulets of aquamarine, associated with the sea god Poseidon, for safety at sea. The Greeks also attributed medicinal properties to various crystals based on their color, building on ancient Babylonian astrological associations between the stones and certain planets.

Both the Greeks and the ancient Romans used amethyst to prevent intoxication when drinking wine. In fact, amethyst gets its name from the Greek word *amethystos*, meaning "not drunk" or "not intoxicated." Roman women used amber amulets for all aspects of childbearing and protection for their children. Roman soldiers brought tiger's eye with them into battle in the belief that it made their armor impervious to the weapons of their enemies.

One famous ancient reference to crystals comes from the Book of Exodus, written in the fifth century BCE. High priests were described wearing a sacred breastplate featuring twelve specific minerals, each of which represented one of the twelve tribes of Israel. According to a biblical passage, there is a specific order of arrangement of these stones and the name of the corresponding tribe was to be inscribed on each one. Because the names of minerals changed over time, it's unclear which exact stones were used in the breastplate, but scholars have suggested that carnelian, lapis lazuli, agate, and amethyst were included. Interestingly, the breastplate also incorporated a set of two objects called the Urim and Thummim, which may have been stones and are believed to have been components of a divination system that was used by the high priest to resolve questions and disputes.

Crystals and European Folk Magic

Much of modern Wicca and other forms of Neopaganism are inspired by what is known about the magical folk traditions of pre-Christian Europe. In addition to the ancient Greeks and Romans, two main cultural groups predominated across Europe for several centuries before the spread of the Christian Church brought massive changes to the pagan world. The Celts occupied much of the central and southern areas of the continent and eventually migrated throughout the British Isles. The Germanic tribes also spread throughout central, western, and northern Europe, along with much of England and parts of Scotland and Ireland. Since both groups were predominantly oral cultures, neither of them left much to work with in terms of written records, which means details about their magical practices are rather scant. However, we can still catch glimpses of how our pagan ancestors viewed and worked with these enchanting pieces of the Earth, thanks to archeological discoveries, myths, and legends handed down over time as well as the folk practices that survived into the Middle Ages and beyond.

Gemstones in Germanic Traditions

Archaeological finds across Europe show that the ancient Germanic peoples used a variety of crystals and mineral stones available in the region. Rune carvings, often used for magical purposes, were glazed with a pigment made from hematite. Sword hilts were sometimes hung with six-sided clear quartz beads, suggesting that the crystal was used for protection and victory in battle. The Vikings also carried almandine, a variety of garnet, into battle for the same purposes.

Many Germanic women used spherical quartz crystal beads for spindle whorls, which would function as prisms as they spun as the cloth was being woven. Other spindle whorls were made from amber and jet, both of which were associated with the goddess Freyja. Since the act of weaving was associated with the creation of fate in Norse mythology, it can be argued that these objects had a symbolic or sacred value beyond their mundane purpose.

The Vikings also made and wore jewelry from quartz, carnelian, amber, and jet as well as gold, bronze, and silver. While many of these pieces were worn for fashion or even as portable currency, it's clear that magical amulets were also widespread, particularly those using clear quartz, amber, and jet. Several of these amulets were associated with the gods Thor and Odin.

One famous scene from Norse mythology describes a völva, or seer, who visits a community in Greenland to tell its future. She carries a staff with her, which is something of an ancestor to the modern Witch's wand. It had a knob made of brass and encrusted with gemstones. For the prophesying ritual, she also wears a blue cloak studded with stones. These details hint at the connection between crystals and the art of divination for which the seeresses of the times were consulted.

According to other stories, stones were also used for healing, for manifesting desires, and even for becoming invisible. One particularly interesting phenomenon was the "sunstone" described in several Icelandic stories, which enabled sailors to navigate far distances at sea on cloudy days by looking for the sun's reflection in it. Scientists now believe that this may have been Iceland spar, or calcite, which polarizes light within its crystal structure and can be used to calculate the direction of the sun. This is an interesting instance of science "catching up" with ancient traditions that had long been dismissed as pure fiction!

Crystals and Stones in the Celtic World

Some have claimed the Druids—the magicians, teachers, and judges of the Celtic tribes—used crystals for healing and in magical rites, but there's not much evidence to support this idea. The belief may be due to a mistaken assumption about the Druid's egg, also known as a serpent's egg or snake stone, which was a talisman described by ancient writers who observed many of the Druids' customs. According to Pliny the Elder, the Druid's egg was a naturally occurring phenomenon created by the secretions of snakes and was used for healing, protection, and success in legal matters, among other things. However, these objects may have been seashells, fossils, or simply egg-shaped stones that were consecrated as talismans for these purposes. It's possible that some Druid's eggs may have been quartz crystals, and this mysterious talisman has also been known as the "Druid's gem" in some Celtic areas. Ultimately, whether the Druids were practitioners of crystal magic remains unclear.

Nonetheless, there is plenty of lore over the centuries regarding crystals and other stones used for folk magic and healing in the Celtic world, particularly in Scotland and Ireland. Amulets to ward off the "evil eye" were made by drilling a hole in the center of a clear quartz stone. Some special stones, like the Cloch-Oir (or Golden Stone), which was said to have been sacred to the Druids, were known as "talking stones" and used as oracles for divination. One tale from the Irish coast tells of a stone used for calming the sea while the fishermen were out in their boats.

There are many tales of "curing stones," which were rubbed on the area of the body where healing was needed or dipped into water which was then drunk by the ill or injured person. These methods were also used on domestic animals, particularly on cattle. Typically, a chant or invocation would accompany the dipping of the stone into the water. While the examples remaining today tend to invoke Christian figures such as the Virgin Mary, they most likely started out as invocations of Celtic deities like Brighid, a goddess of healing.

Quartz crystals were often used for these purposes. They were usually in the shape of round balls or eggs and typically wrapped in bands of silver or gold. Pieces of jet and amber also served as curing stones, along with seashells, flint, and basalt. However, in many cases, the color of the stone appears to have been more important than what the stone was made of. White stones were seen as particularly potent for healing, but one tradition involved finding three green stones in a running stream. Black and red stones were also valued for certain physical ailments.

Some individual crystals were believed to be so powerful that they had names. These were kept within clans and handed down over the generations, and their existence was often well known throughout the community. One example was a silver-wrapped crystal in Scotland known as Clach Donnachaidh, or "victory stone." Another well known stone was a clear crystal orb called Clach na Bratach, or "Stone of the Standard," which belonged to the Clan Robertson since it was discovered by their clan chief in the fourteenth century. The clan carried it into every battle that it fought for the next three hundred years and used it for healing as well as divining the future.

Healing stones could even be found on the altars of many churches in Ireland and Scotland, although Christian authorities were generally eager to stamp out pagan ways. As we will see next, magical ideas about the powers of crystals and mineral stones held sway with plenty of prominent figures in the Church well into the seventeenth century, before eventually fading with the advent of modern science.

Crystals, Christianity, and Science

In today's Wiccan and Pagan communities, the history of our ancestors is often told in a way that suggests that the Christian Church brought paganism to a sudden and near-absolute end in a short period of time. However, as is evident from many documents detailing the use of crystals throughout the Middle Ages, this took several centuries to accomplish, particularly when it came to turning people away from magical beliefs and practices.

Those who converted to Christianity were taught to reject all forms of magic as evil, yet even members of the clergy held what would now be considered "magical" beliefs about crystals, particularly in relation to their healing abilities. The difference was that Christians attributed the natural powers of the stones to the Christian God rather than magic. This belief was no doubt supported by references to crystals and gemstones in the Bible, particularly the twelve stones of the high priest's breastplate discussed on pages 13–14. Whatever the case, it seems that despite the Church's position on magic in general, which became increasingly clear through anti-magic laws passed throughout Europe during the Middle Ages, crystals used for healing purposes were more or less given a pass and were used with enthusiasm by medical healers and bishops alike.

One such healer was a Benedictine abbess named Hildegard von Bingen, who practiced medicine during the twelfth century. In addition to herbs and tinctures, she used various crystals and mineral stones in her practice, including amethyst for insect bites, calcite for stomach issues, and quartz crystal for heart trouble. Agate, jasper, and sapphire were also part of her medicine cabinet. While physical ailments were a primary focus, her remedies also addressed emotional imbalances, irrational tempers, and impractical habits. She was essentially a holistic practitioner, focusing on the spiritual aspects of disease in addition to physical symptoms. As a Christian, she attributed the healing attributes of her crystals to a blessing from God.

The practice of crystal healing was quite common during this era and may have been growing in popularity based on the number of lapidaries (encyclopedia-style books about the properties of crystals and other mineral stones) that were produced in various countries between the eleventh and seventeenth centuries. These books built on the ideas already established by the classical writers of ancient Greece and Rome and emphasized the medicinal value of many different types of stones in addition to their magical properties. And while it was common to attribute the "virtues" of these stones to God, many sources from the Middle Ages show that Christianity had not been completely separated from other belief systems that we might call magical or metaphysical.

For example, Albertus Magnus was a thirteenth-century Catholic bishop and philosopher who wrote many influential works, including *De Mineralibus* (or *Book of Minerals*), in which he describes the purposes of astrological talismans, created by carving zodiac symbols into gems and other stones. A stone inscribed with the sign for Gemini, Libra, or Aquarius, for instance, was said to promote friendship and social harmony. In another work, he recommends wearing diamonds for protection against animal attacks.

Lapidaries from this era also suggest wearing specific gemstones to detect poison, prevent seizures, and ease childbirth. Stones could be magically enhanced by inscribing them with specific letter combinations for protection from sickness. Tables of correspondence for the associations between stones, planets, and zodiac signs were also common.

Another highly influential figure in the world of crystal medicine was Anselmus de Boodt, a Flemish scholar who wrote the

Gemmarum et Lapidum Historia in the beginning of the seventeenth century. His work was considered more scientific than many of the lapidaries of the past, as he was less a believer in magical or "supernatural" powers on the part of the stones and more inclined to credit any healing abilities they might have to their ability to work *with* the body rather than having power *over* it.

He, too, described these abilities as the work of God via the influence of "angels" who would enter the stone to provide healing. He also made more distinctions between stones that had this capacity and stones that were simply the subject of "superstition" and didn't have any effects. De Boodt also wrote about phenomena outside the scope of physical healing. For example, he argued that if wearing turquoise prevents falls, as it was commonly believed, that this effect would also be the work of "an occult agent," with God's permission.

Two major cultural shifts led to the almost complete disappearance of the belief in the inherent magical and healing energies of crystals and stones. The first was the Church's gradual victory over competing faiths among the populations of Europe, which can be seen in many codes of law throughout the region. Church authorities increasingly viewed all folk magic practices as "demonic," and using these practices had legal and religious consequences, resulting in fines and even banishment from the Church. One example of these laws, from thirteenth-century Iceland, relates explicitly to stone magic: "People are not to do things with stones or fill them with magic power with the idea of trying them on people or on livestock. If people put trust in stones to ensure their own health or that of cattle, the penalty is lesser outlawry."

Of course, these laws didn't stop everyone entirely. As late as the nineteenth century, a law was passed in England that promised three month's hard labor for anyone caught using crystals for divination. But by then, the second major cultural shift—the Scientific Revolution, which began in the mid-sixteenth century—was well underway, and discoveries in various fields led to a transformation of how people viewed the natural world. Lapidarists came to conclude that inanimate objects like stones could not possess healing qualities, no matter how visually captivating they might be. Magic as a whole, including the use of crystals in healing, became increasingly relegated to the realm of old-fashioned superstition.

Crystals did appear here and there in various occult revival movements between the eighteenth and twentieth centuries, often in the form of quartz crystal balls used for scrying, but it wasn't until the late twentieth century that they truly made their comeback through the New Age movement. Since then, both crystal healing and crystal magic have been on the rise. It is likely that today, more people are working magic with a larger variety of stones than at any prior point in human history!

So, what are these magical practitioners doing, exactly? What is crystal magic? How does it work? If you are reading this book, you're most likely aware that for all its amazing discoveries, there are some mysteries that modern science has yet to solve. In the case of magic, the scientific method simply isn't set up to measure its results, since they are shaped by the mental focus of the individual working the magic. That said, we can catch glimpses of the way scientific observations overlap with teachings from older wisdom traditions, some of which help illustrate the "how" of crystal magic. We will explore a few angles below.

PRINCIPLES OF CRYSTAL MAGIC

CRYSTAL MAGIC, LIKE ANY OTHER FORM OF MAGIC, IS THE ART of directing a specific intention into the Universe in order to bring about a desired change. While crystal spellwork may make use of various tools, such as candles or herbs, the focal point of this kind of magic will be one or more crystals or other mineral stones. Crystals are unique magical tools in that they occur in nature, but they are not organic like herbs and cannot be cultivated. They are not made by human hands like candles, cauldrons, athames and wands, but they can be sculpted, carved, and polished into beautiful works of art.

Although crystals and stones are made of inorganic matter, many healers who work with them believe them to be "alive," capable of communicating their ancient wisdom with us if we are open and receptive to their messages. Even scientists speak of the process of crystal formation as "growing," since crystals start out small and then increase in size as new atoms are added to their structures under the Earth's surface. The shape, size, and color of a given crystal's formation will depend on the temperature, location, and presence of other minerals, as part of an ancient and ongoing dynamic process of creation. The chemical composition of each type of mineral constitutes a unique energy signature, which we tap into when working with the stones.

Wiccans and other Witches understand that the power of crystals and stones is also in essence the same power inherent in other natural phenomena, such as the wind or a flowing river. All matter, visible and invisible, is essentially energy, and all energy is interconnected. This core concept is found in both metaphysics and quantum physics, and while the exact ways in which energy communicates and ultimately transforms reality remain something of a mystery, we know that our intention, or will, can tap into and even direct those processes. Crystals, as subtle energy conductors, are potent tools for doing so.

Crystals and Universal Energy

While speaking of crystals and energy is typically associated with the metaphysical realm, connections between the two have been observed in conventional science as well.

Certain crystals, such as quartz and tourmaline, exhibit one aspect of their power through what scientists call the *piezoelectric effect*. When mechanical pressure is applied to these stones, for example, by squeezing them or tapping them with a hammer, they give off an observable electric charge. It's this piezoelectricity that helps a quartz watch keep time. Quartz and certain other crystals also exhibit *pyroelectricity*, meaning that they release an electric charge when exposed to a change in temperature. Some healers who use crystals theorize that the stones' healing abilities stem from their piezoelectric and pyroelectric qualities, but in reality, only a few of the crystals most often used in healing and magic are known to exhibit these properties. Nonetheless, every crystal emits its own subtle energy that then interacts with the energy fields of everything around it. Therefore, every crystal responds to the energy flowing through the human body, and when used appropriately, helps to balance that flow and restore it to optimal conditions for good health.

In a magical context, the function of a crystal can be understood through the esoteric wisdom tradition known as the Hermetic Principles. The most relevant for crystal magic is probably the Principle of Vibration, which states that all matter is in constant motion, even though most of it appears to be perfectly still. At the subatomic level, everything is moving and therefore interacting with everything else. The rate, or frequency, at which any piece of matter is vibrating will determine how we perceive it with our senses as well as how its energy interacts with ours. Each crystal vibrates at its own precise frequency, which is determined by its physical makeup, and its vibrations will affect other matter, including the human body. Furthermore, the frequency of a particular crystal will also resonate with the frequencies of a particular condition or situation in life that we wish to change or manifest. For example, rose quartz resonates with frequencies of friendship and love. The bright, sunny energies of citrine resonate with positive vibrations of self-confidence and optimism. Each of these stones, then, are used in magic related to these goals.

Colors are also vibrations of light and resonate with different aspects of our existence (such as love, health, and money matters) according to their specific vibrations. The color of a stone will therefore often have a correspondence with particular magical aims. Pink, the color of rose quartz, is a color with a harmonizing, loving vibration. The color and the physical makeup of this kind of quartz combine to make it a powerful force for drawing love into your life. Likewise, the color green has a vibrational resonance with abundance. Therefore, some green stones, such as bloodstone, are particularly good for spellwork involving matters of prosperity. However, traditional color associations such as those used in Wiccan candle magic are not always consistently applied to crystal-centered magic. For example, citrine and pyrite, both primarily yellow in color, are also associated with prosperity and wealth.

Another way to view the basic makeup of all matter in the Universe is as information or consciousness. The Principle of Mentalism states that at the most basic level, everything is mental, that all of creation stems from the Universal mind. Since thought is energy, the power of thought can shape our reality. It has been established that positive thoughts raise the frequency of one's energetic vibration, while negative thoughts lower it. We can harness this power of thought and use it to send our intentions out into the Universe *through the energy field* of the crystals we choose to work with, utilizing their vibrational frequencies.

Crystals and stones are conduits of energy—our own personal energy as well as that of the Universe. They can receive and transmit Universal energy, acting as powerful agents for the changes we wish to bring forth into manifested reality. They can also assist directly with healing the body and improving the energy of physical spaces, due to their unique inherent energies. They really are incredible representatives of the magic of Nature!

MOVING FORWARD

UNDERSTANDING WHAT CRYSTALS ARE AND WHY THEY MAKE such great magical tools is the first step toward learning how to use them to manifest positive change in your life. The next step, however, is less academic and more experiential—acquiring your own crystals! In the next section, we'll introduce thirteen crystals and stones frequently used in magic. You'll also find tips for choosing and caring for your crystals as well as ways to connect with them energetically for effective use in magic. Get ready to take a hands-on approach to finding and working with your new magical partners!

PART TWO

ACQUAINTING YOURSELF WITH CRYSTALS

YOUR VERY OWN MAGICAL ALLIES

MAGIC IS AN EXPERIENCE OF COCREATION WITH THE NAT-ural energies of the Universe. The magician contributes the intention and specific actions designed to bring about the change. The Universe then works with the intention in the invisible realms, arranging circumstances and events to manifest the magical goal. Crystals, as beings of the Earth with strong vibrational frequencies, are ideal partners for this cocreative process.

In the following pages, you'll be introduced to a "Witch's dozen," or thirteen, of the most potent crystals and mineral stones for working magic. We'll also cover the two major energy types found in all magical stones—projective and receptive energy—and how to begin sensing them. You'll find tips for building your own collection of crystals, regardless of your budget. Caring for your crystals and preparing them for spellwork are essential to magical success, so instructions for cleansing and charging your stones are also provided. Finally, you'll find strategies for incorporating crystals into your daily life in addition to your formal magical practice.

THIRTEEN MAGICAL CRYSTALS

THE EARTH HAS PRODUCED A TRULY STUNNING VARIETY OF crystals and other mineral stones, many of which are wonderful tools in magic as well as healing. This introductory list represents just a few, but they are among the most popular and versatile stones used in various magical traditions around the world. They're also among the most widely available and affordable. Think of this group of stones as a sort of "Witch's starter kit" for crystal magic. Here, you'll find information on each stone's appearance, key energetic properties, and common magical uses.

We'll begin with the best-known crystals within the quartz family, then move to other popular stones with various mineral compositions. As you read through the descriptions, pay attention to any signals from your intuition. You will likely feel drawn to some stones more than others. If so, these are the ideal stones to begin working with first.

Quartz Crystal

The most abundant and arguably the most versatile mineral on the planet, quartz is the one most people associate with the word *crystal*. Usually clear but also opaque white, quartz is used in many magical and non-magical objects including clocks, computers, prisms, crystal spheres, and wands. Quartz is the original source of the word "crystal," which comes from the Greek *krystallos*, meaning "clear ice." The Greeks believed that clear quartz crystal was ice that the deities had made from celestial water that could never be melted.

Clear quartz is a supreme aid in concentration, fostering intellectual clarity, new ideas, and strengthened focus. It increases awareness, helps with memory and filters out external distractions. Interestingly, it is both helpful for sleep and for raising energy, as it has a somewhat hypnotic quality but also contains the full spectrum of light, which can be seen when it's used as a prism. Quartz is a great purifier, helping to eliminate negativity and restore positive energy in a person or in one's surroundings. It's useful in meditation and clearing out inner turmoil, replacing it with positive feelings and affirmations. It assists with perseverance and patience, bringing a sense of purpose and harmony to those who work with its energy.

Clear quartz is a very versatile stone, easy to "program" (or charge) with magical intention for any positive purpose. It stores and concentrates the energy, retaining it for use in healing and magic at a later time. This crystal serves to amplify the power of your intentions as well as the power of other stones used along with it in ritual. It is particularly well suited for communication with spirit guides, building psychic ability, communication with animals and plants, and recalling past lives. Many people use quartz in workings connected to strengthening intuition and spiritual development. It also works well for attracting love and prosperity. Wearing or carrying a clear quartz crystal helps keep personal energy strong and positive, and the mind and heart open to guidance from the higher realms. It dispels negative energy from others in your environment. Placing quartz in the bath is a good way to unwind and clear your mind when facing confusing events.

KEY WORDS: Clarity, transformation, manifestation
ZODIAC SIGN: Leo
PLANET: Sun
ELEMENT: Fire
ENERGY: Receptive

Rose Quartz

A pink variety of quartz crystal, rose quartz is universally associated with love and relationships, including friendship. In Greek legend, Eros, the god of love, brought this stone to the people of Earth in hopes of inspiring love among them and dissipating the anger that caused them to remain lonely and apart from one another. It has been used in love talismans since ancient times, often carved into hearts and given as a gift to a loved one. Rose quartz can vary slightly in appearance, from translucent to opaque pink, and the brightness of the color can depend on the amount of sun exposure the crystal has experienced. However, even the palest of these stones has great power.

Rose quartz has a nurturing energy and is good for recovering from emotional upset. It strengthens compassion and the ability to forgive others for past wrongs, which is necessary for inner peace and for attracting positive, healthy relationships. It promotes the ability to accept yourself just as you are and to accept others just as they are. Rose quartz is good for spellwork devoted to all things bad break, including the love of friendship, whether you're working to bring new love into your life or heal from old relationship issues. It's also helpful for

grounding yourself after spellwork or divination. Placed by the bed, it promotes the restoration of trust and harmony and is great for both children and adults as a sleep crystal. Place one under a child's pillow to relieve nightmares or fear of the dark. Rose quartz is also a good crystal to have near your computer, as it helps prevent eye fatigue and resulting headaches. Adding it to a magical bath promotes feelings of overall well-being and release from emotional troubles.

KEY WORDS: Love, self-awareness, balance, transformation
ZODIAC SIGN: Taurus
PLANET: Venus
ELEMENT: Earth
ENERGY: Receptive

Amethyst

Another form of quartz crystal, amethyst is considered by many to be the most beautiful of magical stones. It ranges in color from pale lavender to deep, very dark purple and may be transparent or opaque. The color is created by the presence of manganese in clear quartz, and the variation in hue is caused by additional amounts of iron. Amethyst frequently occurs in geodes, where it is common to see amethyst and clear quartz points clustered together.

In ancient Greece, amethyst was considered the "stone of sobriety," believed to help reduce the intoxicating effects of wine. To this day, it is used in working to break addictions as well as other unwanted habits and patterns. Amethyst has a very high vibration that helps people connect to their spiritual selves and find the balance between healthy indulgences and unhealthy overindulgence. It is a stone of contentment, aiding in meditation and attaining higher states of consciousness and transforming negative energy into positive energy. It also helps enhance perception on both intellectual and intuitive levels and increases psychic ability.

In magic, amethyst is wonderful for clearing sacred space and maintaining a positive atmosphere anywhere it is placed. It is useful for healing rituals related to addiction of all kinds, both physical and emotional (such as difficulty removing oneself from toxic relationships). It increases luck and prosperity by curbing the tendency to overspend and promoting motivation. It's a good stone for creativity and any projects requiring imaginative thinking and focus. Amethyst has been used traditionally in Wiccan magic for dispelling illusion and to bring about psychic healing.

Wearing or carrying amethyst creates a protective shield against negative energies in your environment. Like rose quartz, amethyst near the computer can help relieve eyestrain, and it's also a good stone to keep under your pillow for peaceful dreams. Unpolished amethyst is a good charger for other crystals and provides healing energy for plants—place it in areas where plants don't tend to thrive to purify the energy and enhance their growth.

KEY WORDS: Transformation, higher guidance, protection
ZODIAC SIGN: Aquarius
PLANET: Jupiter
ELEMENT: Air
ENERGY: Receptive

Citrine

Citrine is a yellow variety of quartz. It is usually transparent and ranges in color from pale yellow to gold though it is sometimes found in an almost-brown honey color. It has been known as the "Sun Stone" due to its bright color and often sparkling appearance, but the name *citrine* comes from the French word for lemon. It is said that citrine never absorbs or accumulates negative energy, but instead "zaps" it up and releases it as positive energy. This is true for both physical and subtle energy levels so that citrine can brighten up a space or a mood simply through its ability to transform negativity into positivity.

With its sunny, endlessly positive energy, citrine is a great energizer and motivator, strengthening your connection to yourself and your ability to manifest your desires. It promotes clarity of thought, enhanced creativity, and encourages self-expression, helping you to visualize your goals clearly and bring them "into the daylight." It raises self-esteem and self-confidence, clearing the path for more direct action toward your goals. Citrine helps overcome fear and depression and encourages new approaches to problems and enthusiasm for new experiences.

Citrine is also good for helping to overcome negativity associated with having been ill-used by another person, either through direct manipulation or subtler means. It can be hard sometimes to know whether some acquaintances are positive influences in our lives. Citrine can help illuminate which of your associations are worth keeping and which to let go. It can do this for your own thoughts as well by clearing out negative or unnecessary mental "chatter" to help you realign with your inner wisdom. It reduces sensitivity to criticism and helps you let go of the past, clearing the way for new positive thoughts and experiences.

Citrine is excellent in spellwork for manifesting and maintaining wealth. It is sometimes known as the "Merchant's Stone" and kept near the cash register of many businesses. It's also good for issues of communication in interpersonal relationships as well as clearing and blocking negative energies from people around you. Wear or carry citrine as a general protection against negativity to attract money or guard against excessive spending and in any situation where you need to feel secure and confident.

KEY WORDS: Clarity, manifestation, clearing, willpower
ZODIAC SIGN: Gemini
PLANET: Mercury
ELEMENT: Air
ENERGY: Projective

Moonstone

Moonstone is named for its opaque, silver, and white sheen reminiscent of the moon, although it can be found in a variety of colors, including blue, gray, peach. There is even a multicolored variety called "Rainbow Moonstone." Associated with the element of Water, it has a feminine quality that helps you tap into your inner wisdom and psychic abilities. It is also known as the "Traveler's Stone" and has long been a talisman of safe journeys, though these journeys may be inward, soul-searching travels as well as physical journeys to a faraway location.

This stone's affinity with the Moon makes it ideal for connecting to the regular cycles of and natural rhythms of life, reminding us that there is a time for all things and that allowing for right timing is often better than trying to force things to happen on our preferred schedules. It has a calming energy that reminds us to stay in the present moment and open up to the joy available to us when we let go of the chatter of the mind and listen to the heart instead. In a culture where we feel pressured to "know the answers" and "be in control" of our circumstances, moonstone helps us relax into the mysteries of the future, developing our intuition and staying open to possibilities we can't see yet with our rational minds.

In Wiccan magic, moonstone has been used to increase psychic abilities and clairvoyance, relieve stress and foster compassion, and to accompany ritual worship of triple moon-goddesses. It's also a good stone for spellwork related to female reproductive health and childbirth as well as erotic love and kundalini energies. Although it is ultrafeminine in its energy, it is not just a woman's stone; it helps men tune into their own feminine side and encourages them to open up to more creative thinking and emotional balance. It's also another good stone for encouraging restful sleep, particularly in children and especially when on a trip away from home. It is still worn as a talisman when traveling, particularly at night and/or on journeys over water. Some people keep a moonstone in the glove compartment of their car, and it is said to be good protection against road rage.

KEY WORDS: Clarity, higher guidance, intuition
ZODIAC SIGN: Cancer
PLANET: Moon
ELEMENT: Water
ENERGY: Receptive

Carnelian

With its rich red-orange-to-orange coloring, carnelian was known to the ancient Egyptians as "the setting sun." Single pieces of this stone can include several shades between red-orange and golden yellow and are sometimes streaked with white. Used in Egyptian magic as protection against the evil eye, it was also carried by the Romans for protection and courage. Carnelian's energy is bold, joyful, encouraging, and empowering, making it a great stone for any situation in which you need a strong boost of positive personal power.

Carnelian also has a grounding influence, helping to anchor us in the present moment and therefore make better use of the high-level energy it provides. It can calm anger and replace it with new enthusiasm for life. Its energy is good for endurance, motivation, courage, and passion—traits that bring success in whatever endeavor you're hoping to succeed in. It helps overcome procrastination and helps you move from the dreaming/planning phase of a project to the action required to get it done. Creative types can benefit from carnelian's ability to move past creative blocks and manifest one's inner vision in the outer world, particularly when one's "inner critic" is the main obstacle. Carnelian helps those struggling with indecision to make a choice and act on it, bringing them closer to achieving their goals.

Wiccans have long recognized carnelian's assistance with grounding and aligning with one's spiritual guides, and it makes a good talisman against "psychic attack," or negative thoughts projected by others. It's also good for spellwork related to love and to invigorating a relationship with new sexual passion. As a motivator and activator, it is said to attract prosperity and is good for money-making ventures. Some use it to guard their homes from theft, storms, fires, or other damage. It is also known as the "Singer's Stone" and can promote confidence in people performing on stage. Most often, however, it is worn to enhance desire, passion, and love.

KEY WORDS: Grounding, self-awareness, creativity, vitality
ZODIAC SIGN: Leo
PLANET: Sun
ELEMENT: Fire
ENERGY: Projective

Bloodstone

Also called heliotrope, bloodstone is a deep, earthy green stone, usually speckled with bright-to-brownish red and sometimes gold. The green may also range from greenish-blue to greenish-black and may be translucent or opaque, depending on where it is found. Bloodstone gets its name from a myth about the crucifixion of Christ—that some of Christ's blood fell on some green jasper stones. Some specimens may almost entirely lack the red inclusions, but holding bloodstone up to bright light can reveal colors not seen in ordinary light.

Bloodstone is a powerful crystal for blasting through negative, distracting, or excessive emotions to get to the truth of a situation. It helps to calm the mind and dispel confusion for better decision-making. Its energy is practical, strong, and grounding, and it is good for helping you return to the present moment after worrying too much about the future or regretting the past. This makes it a good stone for heightening intuition, as we can only really hear our inner wisdom when we are still and centered in the present.

Bloodstone has been used in magic to reduce emotional and mental stress, stimulate kundalini energy, and psychic healing. It is also used in rituals to honor the Goddess and for seeking information about past lives from dreams. Many use bloodstone as an aid in banishing negative energy as well as in weather magic, drawing on the power of a strong wind or rainstorm to increase strength and courage or wash away unwanted habits or patterns. It's good for fertility and attracting money, and excellent for manifesting healing of all kinds. Wear or carry it to increase mental clarity and calm the mind and for strength when adjusting to change. As a booster of energy levels, bloodstone is also good for physical endurance and makes a good luck charm for those involved in sports competitions.

KEY WORDS: Clearing, protection, vitality
ZODIAC SIGN: Aries
PLANET: Mars
ELEMENT: Fire
ENERGY: Projective

Jade

For nearly 6,000 years, jade has been a prized stone used in tools, ritual artifacts, and jewelry from ancient Britain to Central and South America to New Zealand and China. This stone is normally green and mostly opaque, though it can be somewhat translucent and occur in shades of white, gray, and pink. It has traditionally been a symbol of tranquility, truthfulness, wisdom, and luck.

On the emotional and spiritual planes, jade is a great stone for helping you to tap into your authentic self, the self that knows what is best for you underneath all the emotional chaos that may be occurring during a difficult or confusing time. It helps with self-trust and with clearing away past emotional experiences that cloud your ability to see  the present circumstances objectively. It also helps you to be your real self in your interactions with others, rather than trying to present yourself in a way that you think will be pleasing to them. For these reasons, jade has a very calming energy and is excellent help for unsettling situations in your life. It also leads to the ability to create better circumstances—in terms of relationships, health, wealth, and new opportunities—because you're aligning your goals with your authentic self. It can also help make difficult tasks feel easier to accomplish, increasing your sense of peace around work.

Jade is used in magical workings for protection, eliminating negativity and tapping into our innate wisdom and courage. It is used as a "dream stone" to bring insight from the spiritual realms by placing it on the forehead at the location of the "third eye." Keeping it under your pillow can help you remember your dreams better. As a green stone, the color of prosperity, jade can also be used in spellwork for abundance, and it helps plants grow. It supports new love and harmony in business relationships as well as within the family. Some people keep a piece or two of jade in their workplace to keep away unwanted negativity from coworkers. Carry a piece in your pocket to help recharge your energy; it is also believed to invigorate the immune system.

KEY WORDS: Self-awareness, transformation, manifestation
ZODIAC SIGN: Pisces
PLANET: Neptune
ELEMENT: Water
ENERGY: Receptive

Lapis Lazuli

Also known as lazurite and sometimes shortened to just lapis, this beautiful stone is found in many shades from pale blue to deep, nearly indigo blue, and often has white streaks and gold inflections. It was extremely valuable to the ancient Egyptians and Sumerians, connected to the divine through its association with the blue of the sky. Lapis is associated with truth, communication, and connection to higher wisdom.

Energetically, lapis lazuli is good for lifting depression and restoring a sense of inner peace. Like jade, it is a stone of self-knowledge and helps you reflect on how your perceptions and beliefs shape your decisions. It stimulates intuition and motivation, making it easier to manifest circumstances that you desire and that are for your highest good. For people who are consciously tending their spiritual journey, this stone helps maintain connection with the higher self and access to inspiration from the spiritual plane. Lapis also works on the intellectual level, activating our desire for knowledge and understanding, helping us to integrate new knowledge, and enhancing memory. As a stone of truth, lapis helps you communicate honestly and effectively, both with others and with yourself. This property makes it a great stone for aid in written communication as well. Holding a piece of lapis to the third eye or in your hand while meditating can help you increase your ability to quickly register what your truth is and give you the confidence to express it.

Wiccans have used lapis to increase psychic abilities and establish clear contact with their higher selves. This stone is also great for workings to strengthen love relationships and friend-ships as well as to restore balance and harmony between our egos and our deeper selves. It is an ideal stone for spellwork done out-doors under the night sky and for receiving prophetic information in dreams. Wear or carry lapis when approaching communication of all kinds, whether a meaningful conversation between friends or a public speaking occasion. It can also protect against negative words or thoughts from others, returning that energy to its source.

KEY WORDS: Higher guidance, intuition, communication
ZODIAC SIGN: Libra
PLANET: Jupiter
ELEMENT: Air
ENERGY: Receptive and projective

Malachite

Another stone revered by the ancients, malachite was used by the Greeks and Romans for ornaments, jewelry, and, in powdered form, for eyeshadow. (This last use turned out to be a bad idea since malachite is toxic and should *never* be used as a powder. Polished malachite pieces are the safest bet.) Malachite is an opaque stone of deep, rich green with lighter green circular bands that cause many pieces to appear to have an eye. For this reason, the stone was believed in the Middle Ages to ward off negativity and enhance visionary abilities.

Malachite is considered a "Stone of Transformation," fostering spiritual growth during times of great change or inspiring us to make important changes and take emotional risks. Its energy can help you break unwanted patterns that restrict your growth, such as avoiding social situations due to shyness or self-consciousness. This stone helps build emotional courage and clarity by helping us learn to recognize and then release old emotional wounds, especially those suffered in childhood. It helps with fear of confrontation, encourages expression of feelings, and promotes healthy, positive relationships and empathy for others.

Malachite is good for protection magic, particularly for people who get easily overwhelmed by the congestion of psychic energy in crowded places. It's good for all travel situations and is particularly helpful if you have a fear of flying. It absorbs negative energy, so holding it in the palm of your hand during difficult or frightening situations can bring immediate relief, but be sure to clean and clear it often if you use it for this purpose. As a green stone, it can be used in any prosperity spell, and it is also good in workings for healing emotional wounds. In the workplace, it helps dispel energetic toxins from fluorescent lighting, electrical equipment, and unwanted noise.

KEY WORDS: Self-awareness, healing, clarity, protection
ZODIAC SIGN: Scorpio
PLANET: Venus
ELEMENT: Earth
ENERGY: Receptive

Tiger's Eye

Tiger's eye is a beautiful stone of light to dark brown with gold highlights and dark brown to black banding, which, when polished, resembles the shimmering stripes of a tiger and creates a similar "eye" effect to that of malachite. As an "eye stone," it was regarded by the ancient Egyptians and Romans as a stone of protection as well as "second sight," allowing its wearer to see beyond the physical limits of doors and walls.

The energy of tiger's eye is excellent for soothing and resolving emotional turmoil, as it helps you observe emotional patterns from a more distant, objective standpoint. Witnessing the larger picture of a situation, including the viewpoints and circumstances of others involved, facilitates the release of emotions that may be blocking your ability to leave the situation behind and move into higher levels of consciousness.

Tiger's eye is also helpful in this regard for its ability to help you separate fantasy (which arises from emotion) from the reality of a situation. This energy is good for helping you gather focus and renewed energy when pursuing a goal, especially one that is relatively long-term and complex. It promotes courage, strength, and the ability to see things with true optimism.

Magical uses for tiger's eye include invigorating overall energy and physical health as well as in spellwork for courage and self-confidence. It's good in rituals related to emotional clarity and for protection and grounding. Its ability to keep you in touch with reality also makes it good for prosperity, as it helps curb temptations toward gambling or other forms of impulsive spending and improves the ability to attract wealth through practicality and focus. Many people carry tiger's eye for good luck as well as for increased psychic "radar" to cut through any deceptions or illusions created by others. Additionally, those with affinities for tigers and other big cats have used this tiger's eye as a prayer stone for the animals' conservation and well-being in the wild and in sanctuaries.

KEY WORDS: Clarity, balance, vitality
ZODIAC SIGN: Capricorn, Leo
PLANET: Sun
ELEMENT: Earth, Fire
ENERGY: Projective

Jet

One of the exceptions to the "rule" defining crystals and stones, jet is not technically a mineral but fossilized driftwood that has decayed under extreme pressure to become a form similar to coal. It is surprisingly lightweight and warms quickly in the palm of your hand. Jet was mined as early as 1500 BCE and was used in pendants and as beads in ancient times. It was believed to protect against illness and attacks from personal enemies.

As a stone of transmutation—having begun as one substance and ended as another—jet is helpful for transitions. Its energy appeals to mental cloudiness, helping you ground and center yourself to see clearly your best possible approach to changing circumstances. When the future is unknown, it can be hard to maintain clarity of focus as we become uncomfortable about being unable to see exactly what's ahead. Jet helps clear the fog of this anxiety and sets us up to stay open to positive possibilities. This stone absorbs energy from negative thinking and, as such, should be cleaned often if used for this purpose. It is also a great meditation stone, helping to increase spiritual awareness and to heal from grief and sorrow.

Jet is considered one of the most protective magical stones, used for guarding a home against negative energies and to banish unwanted spirits. It has been traditionally used to protect against damage from thunderstorms, and the wives of sailors wear it to protect their husbands at sea. It is used in spellwork to guard against nightmares, violence, and psychic vampires. Some Witches place it on their altars to increase the effectiveness of whatever magic they're working. As a black stone working on the mental level, it is good for increased psychic awareness as well as divination.

KEY WORDS: Clarity, grounding, transformation, wisdom
ZODIAC SIGN: Capricorn
PLANET: Saturn
ELEMENT: Earth
ENERGY: Receptive

Hematite

Hematite is a silvery dark gray stone, very shiny when polished and widely used today in jewelry, such as bracelets and anklets, to help soothe the symptoms of arthritis. It gets its name from the Greek word for blood, because the stone turns red in powdered form. This characteristic is hinted at in another name for the stone—iron rose. In fact, the powdered form of hematite was used as one of the earliest pigments in ancient cave paintings.

Hematite's calming, grounding energy can be experienced as noticeably "heavy," and it is one of the easiest stones to sense

immediately upon holding it. It draws focus away from the mind and into the body, helping you stay connected to the Earth and in the present moment. Once you are grounded and centered, it's easier to handle tasks that require mental organization, such as mathematics and logical thinking. Hematite decreases negativity, further helping to integrate mind, body, and spirit, and enhances self-confidence and self-esteem.

Magically, hematite is used for protection, divination, and psychic awareness. It can be placed in the corners of a room or even in the corners of a yard to protect the space from negativity. It's good for grounding during spiritual work, keeping you connected to the Earth plane during your astral journey so that reintegrating into consensual reality is an easier, smoother process. Many Witches use hematite in spellwork related to confidence and willpower and solving complex problems. As a divination tool, you can hold a large piece of hematite near a candle and watch the images created by the flame's reflection in the surface. It's also great for preparing for magic. If you want to do some spellwork but are unable to get yourself in the right mental space, try meditating while holding or wearing hematite for several minutes to calm the energy of the distracted mind.

KEY WORDS: Grounding, protection, clearing, stability
ZODIAC SIGN: Capricorn, Aries
PLANET: Saturn
ELEMENT: Fire, Earth, Water
ENERGY: Projective

CRYSTAL ENERGIES:
PROJECTION AND RECEPTION

AS YOU BEGIN EXPERIMENTING WITH YOUR NEW CRYSTALS, you'll want to spend time tuning to the unique vibrational frequencies of each stone. You may find that some are easier to "feel" in a noticeable way than others, at least at first. There are many possible reasons for this, but one likely explanation is that you're interacting with two different types of energy known to magical practitioners as *projective* and *receptive* energies. Learning to feel these subtle energies helps you strengthen your connection with your crystals and gain a more intuitive sense of which stones best serve any given purpose.

Like the concept of yin and yang in Chinese philosophy, projective and receptive energies are fundamental to the makeup of the Universe, and each serves equally important purposes in magic. Like the energies of night and day, masculine and feminine, and the waxing and waning phases of the Moon, the energetic quality of any given stone is significant to the spell being worked.

Projective Stones

Projective energies can be likened to the yang energy described in traditional Chinese medicine. These are masculine energies, often characterized as being or feeling strong, bright, physical, active, electric, and hot. The colors of projective stones tend to be associated with strong sunlight—red, yellow, orange and gold. They often emit a "charged" feeling, which can range from subtle to quite "buzzy," depending on the type of stone and the level of receptivity of the person holding it. This is because they send—or project—energy outward. This capacity can be harnessed magically in a few different ways. You can use a projective stone to send positive energy to you or to someone else (with their permission). You can also use it to repel negative energy so that the energy it projects acts as a shield, somewhat like how two like ends of a magnet repel each other.

Projective stones are ideal for magic involving healing and protection from unwanted energy. They are associated with the masculine Elements of Fire and Air, which also makes them good choices for working for vitality, courage, and intellectual power. Projective stones affect the conscious mind and are great to carry with you when you're feeling a need for strength, determination, willpower, or self-confidence. Some popular projective stones include amber, bloodstone, carnelian, citrine, garnet, red jasper, onyx, and tiger's eye.

Receptive Stones

Receptive energies can be said to correspond with the yin energy of the Chinese system and are described as feminine energies, which may be experienced as calm, inward, spiritual, passive, magnetic, and cold. Colors of receptive stones are cooler colors, such as green, blue, purple, silver, and gray. (Pink stones, although they come at the beginning of the color spectrum, are also generally receptive, as the color is more calming than energizing when compared to red or orange.) Holding a receptive stone in your hand is almost guaranteed to make you feel calmer, because the stone is *receiving* the anxious energy from your body, drawing it away from you. (Of course, as with projective stones, this effect will vary from stone to stone and person to person.) This capacity to draw energy inward can be harnessed magically to attract what you desire, such as good luck, love, positive vibrations, or prosperity into your life. It can also be used to draw away from you what you don't desire, like sadness or toxic vibrations.

Associated with the feminine Elements of Earth and Water, receptive stones are great for meditation and emotional and physical grounding as well as promoting psychic abilities. They are good for working on the subconscious mind and may be used in spellwork for love, compassion, peace, and spiritual development. Some receptive stones include jade, lapis lazuli, malachite, moonstone, opal, rose quartz, and turquoise.

Dual-Energy Stones

Most minerals fall into either the receptive or projective category, though there are some that hold both types within their energy signature. For example, quartz crystal can exhibit both, depending on what it's being used for, and because it's a highly "programmable" stone, the user can choose which kind of energy to draw on prior to charging it for spellwork. Some Witches attribute this dual quality to amethyst, lapis lazuli, opal, and cross stone (andalusite) as well. Furthermore, stones that are black in color may be projective or receptive, depending on their type.

Don't worry if you can't tell right away whether a crystal is projective, receptive, or a mix of both. You can usually find this information with a little research, though even then you might find different answers for certain stones, as not all practitioners will experience the energy of a given mineral in the same way. Ultimately, it is your personal experience with your crystals that counts the most when it comes to using them in magic. As you practice holding and attuning to crystals and stones, you will become more adept at noting what kind of energy you're interacting with and what kinds of magic your stones might help you with.

BUILDING YOUR MAGICAL CRYSTAL COLLECTION

THE PROSPECT OF ACQUIRING YOUR OWN CRYSTALS AND stones can seem daunting at first. Many beginners to crystal magic think they need to go out and buy a big collection of various stones. This can be especially tempting if you're lucky enough to live near a shop that specializes in mineral stones! However, this approach is not recommended. For one thing, it can be quite costly. More importantly, however, it takes time to connect energetically with every crystal that comes into your life. Bringing home ten or more new stones all at once may end up being more energetically overwhelming than rewarding, so it is ideal to start with just a few.

If you haven't already, start looking for shops in your area that may carry crystals. Many Wiccan-related shops at least have collections of small polished stones that are common in magical workings. Other types of New Age stores will carry a variety as well and may also offer larger-sized raw crystals and geodes. There are also some shops entirely devoted to crystals and other minerals, where you can find an astounding variety of stones from around the globe in every shape and size imaginable. Of course, if there are none of these types of stores in your area, there are plenty of quality online retailers. With some research and careful consideration, you can have your first magical stones on their way to you in no time!

Ethical Buying

Speaking of research, it's important to acknowledge some ethical considerations when it comes to buying crystals. As noted in part one, crystals and other minerals have become unprecedentedly popular since the resurgence of crystal healing within the New Age movement. This phenomenon, combined with the explosion of interest in Wicca and magic in the twenty-first century, has created an equally unprecedented demand for these items, which has spilled over even into mainstream

commercial realms like department stores and corporate fashion chains. Unfortunately, this means that the incentive for mining and processing crystals at a fast and profitable rate has also increased, which often leads to unethical practices.

The main concerns here are the same as they've always been when it comes to mining: environmental destruction and unsafe and unfair labor practices. For large mining operations, profit is often more important than treating workers and the Earth itself with appropriate care. This can also be true when it comes to lapidaries—the factories where mineral stones are polished before they go to market. The workers who tumble the stones into shining beauties may receive very low wages or work in conditions that are unsafe for their lungs.

Ideally, crystal dealers could choose only to work with mines and lapidaries where ethical standards are taken seriously and even set up a system for certifying crystals as "fair trade." But it's pretty hard to trace where any given stone really came from. This can be due to trade secrets, meaning that mine owners want to keep their specific locations hidden from competitors or due to wholesalers (the middlemen) that are not always honest about which mines they're dealing with. Furthermore, many minerals used in magic and healing are not valuable enough in comparison to industrial minerals, such as copper, for miners to go after on their own. Without the bigger industrial mines extracting them as by-products, we might not have access to the variety of stones we enjoy today.

The bottom line is that your crystals may have changed hands many times before they arrived in the shop where you bought them, and no one may know for sure whether they were mined in an ethical manner. That said, with a little research, you can find out whether the retailer you're dealing with has made any effort to work with ethical suppliers. Start by looking online for more information about what makes a mining operation or lapidary "ethical," and for online crystal retailers who address this topic. Scour the websites of any online or in-person retailer you're thinking of buying from and see if they offer information about where their minerals are sourced or the wholesalers they do business with. Some larger mineral retailers in the United States own and operate their own mines, and they may be more likely to have acceptable standards than mines in poorer regions of the world.

You may find that many retailers simply say they trust their sources, but those who are truly committed will provide more extensive information and be as transparent as possible. If there's no mention of ethical sourcing at all, then it's reasonable to assume they aren't making much effort, but you can still contact them and ask directly. When shopping in person, ask the store clerks what they know about the sources of their crystals and engage them in conversation about ethical buying. If they're unaware of the topic or seem to respond negatively to your questions, that may be a good sign that this isn't the best place for you to get your stones.

In the end, as with anything, go with your intuition. If you feel called to do business with a specific retailer, follow that. If you just really want a rose quartz but don't sense a good energetic connection to the sourcing of it, be patient and try another store or website. At the very least, avoid buying crystals from big-box stores or other places that have nothing to do with magic or healing. Try to support businesses devoted to spiritual pursuits or mineral stores that follow ethical practices.

Crystals on a Budget

Once you start looking at commercially available crystals, the options can be dizzying. Many shops sell beautifully carved stone pieces, such as hearts carved from rose quartz or intricate animal figurines carved from softer stones like malachite or jet. These pieces can make wonderful talismans. You'll also likely find several varieties of polished crystal points, which are good tools for directing energy in very specific ways.

However, it's not necessary to spend money on these fancier items to create successful magic. Keep in mind that a stone in its raw form is every bit as magical as a carved and polished piece, even if raw stones might appear somewhat unglamorous in comparison. Some crystal healers find that raw stones are more energetically potent, and this can be true when using them in certain types of magic as well. Furthermore, larger crystals can easily run into the hundreds of dollars, depending on the type, so don't be overly concerned about size. Most smaller stones are available for around five dollars or less, so if you keep it small and simple, you can get more variety for your budget.

It's important to note that buying from stores isn't the only way to acquire crystals. Great finds can be made at yard sales and flea markets, and you might also do some research into the geology of your area to see what kinds of minerals might be discovered there. This will depend on where you live, of course, but it's not unheard of to find a good specimen of crystal or other mineral in a streambed or your backyard.

You can also work some magic to call stones into your life. A spell for this purpose is included in part three on page 79. Be sure to thank the Universe and any deities or other allies you work with when the stone appears. Sometimes, friends who also work with stones may pass one along to you. When this happens, you'll know the stone has chosen you without any effort on your part!

You need to invest time and energy and attention to work successful magic, but you definitely don't need to invest more money than you can afford. Make it a goal to acquire one or two stones at first and then add gradually to your collection as you see fit. Remember that the quality of your connection to your stones will affect the outcome of any magical workings you do with them, so it's worth taking this journey slowly, one or two stones at a time.

Choosing, Being Chosen, and Letting Go

Many who work magic with crystals and stones will tell say that the stones choose you rather than the other way around. When you buy from a brick-and-mortar shop, you may be the one making the selection, but you are likely to be drawn to particular stones without consciously thinking about it. You may feel pulled strongly toward a certain color or type of stone. Sometimes the choice becomes suddenly obvious, while at other times, you may need to hold a few different stones for a while to get a feel for which one would be best for you. Place the stone in the palm of your dominant hand, then place your other palm on top. Hold the stone gently—don't squeeze—and take a deep breath. Take a moment to scan your physical body and your emotional energy. How do you feel at your center? If you have a positive feeling, this may be the stone for you. If you have any kind of negative feeling, then it is not. Stones aren't harmful in and of themselves and don't give off "negative" energy, but if it's really not a good fit, they may let you know rather strongly.

If you're purchasing crystals from an online business, you don't have the luxury of physically examining your choices. However, you can often contact the proprietors with any questions you may have. You might even let them know that you're just beginning to work with crystals, your intended purpose for them, or anything else you feel would help you make more informed choices about the number and type of stones you'd like to acquire. Again, you can also work some magic to help ensure the right stones are sent to you. Light a candle and speak your intentions, using the spell on page 79, or a working of your own devising. You might even direct your spell words at the stones themselves so that they make themselves known to the employee selecting them for you.

As you build your collection of crystals and stones, beware of what some call "spiritual hoarding." If your space becomes cluttered with crystals (or any other magical objects, for that matter), you will be reducing the beneficial effects of having them in your possession. You can tell this is happening if you're looking around your room and find yourself a little stressed or even annoyed by the sight of all the stones, no matter how bright and sparkly they may be. If you're having a hard time finding a good place for each of your crystals to occupy in your home, that's typically a sign that you have too many at the moment.

You could pack some away in order to reduce visual clutter, but that won't necessarily take care of energetic disharmony. So be open to letting go of a few of your treasures from time to time. Gift them to friends, return them to the Earth, or leave them outside somewhere for someone else to find. You can also work banishing magic with stones that you're ready to let go of, which you'll then bury somewhere away from your home. An example of a banishing spell using crystals is on page 97.

Even if you're not having a clutter issue, you may occasionally become aware that a particular crystal or stone in your possession doesn't quite "belong" with you anymore. You may get a slightly strange feeling about it, or feel downright uncomfortable when you look at it. This is often a sign that the stone is ready to go to someone else or even be returned to the Earth. However, if this happens with a stone you're not very familiar with or haven't had for long, do some research first to find out what its healing and magical qualities are. Sometimes, the stone just wants to teach you something about bringing an aspect of your life back into balance. Alternatively, you may learn that the stone could be helpful to someone you know for a particular reason and know who to give it to.

INTEGRATING CRYSTALS INTO YOUR MAGICAL PRACTICE

ONCE YOU'VE BROUGHT A NEW CRYSTAL INTO YOUR HOME, you'll want to take some steps to intentionally integrate it into your life. After all, the stone won't do much for you if you simply place it on a shelf and ignore it. First, you'll need to clean and clear it of any unwanted energy. This is always important with any magical items, but it's particularly advisable to do it sooner rather than later when it comes to crystals, as they emit energy into your space in a uniquely palpable way.

Before using it for any healing or spellwork, you'll need to charge the stone with your own personal magical energy. It's also ideal to spend some time getting to know your new magical ally before putting it to work in a spell. Following the steps outlined here will increase the power of all the work you do with your new crystals and stones. You'll find details and tips for each on the following pages.

Cleaning and Clearing

If you were able to spend some time holding different stones as you were making your selection in the shop, then chances are that countless others may have also held the very stone you've brought into your home. Even if this isn't the case, the stone has most likely been handled by several people throughout the process of being mined and then transported from its place of origin. The energies of these people can be thought of almost as spiritual "germs." While these traces of energy are unlikely to be harmful to you, they do need to be removed to clear the way for charging the stone with your own energy. This is especially true of stones that may have been mined or processed unethically.

This section covers a few different methods for cleaning and clearing your stones. Note that while one is not necessarily more effective than another, some methods are not recommended for certain stones, depending on their physical makeup and their degree of hardness. You may feel drawn to a particular method, or you may wish to experiment to find what's best for you. If you're unsure about the best method for a particular stone, do some research just to be on the safe side.

Perhaps the simplest way to clean a crystal or stone is with water, which works on both the physical and subtle energy levels. In a pinch, you can just hold the stone under running tap water for several minutes, visualizing all unwanted energy being washed away down the drain. This is not the most environmentally friendly method, however, so you might want to reserve it for when you're just removing dust, which can be done much more quickly. Note that for some minerals, such as mica and selenite, water is destructive, so if you're unsure whether your stone should get wet, do some research first. A small brush is a good alternative for dust removal, particularly for a geode or other stone with a complex texture.

For energetic clearing, a great alternative to tap water is a natural source of running water. If you're lucky enough to have access to a river or stream, you can place the stones in a mesh bag or hold them carefully in your hands as you thank the water for carrying away the unwanted energy. You can also fill a bowl with purified water and set the stones in it for a few hours. Some people like to add sea salt to the water first, particularly for cleaning and clearing quartz crystal, but this is harmful method for many other stones. Aqua aura, for example, deteriorates in salt water. Again, look up any stones you're unsure about, and avoid leaving any stones in saltwater for more than a few hours.

Another way to use nature's elemental gifts to clean crystals is leaving them in sunlight for several hours. Sunlight both cleans and charges stones at the same time, simplifying the process! It is ideal to leave them outside, but placing them in a windowsill also works well. You may want to repeat this for two or three days, until your crystals are absolutely sparkling. This is particularly good for red, orange, and yellow stones such as carnelian and citrine. However, be aware that some stones will fade in direct sunlight over time. This is particularly true for transparent, colored crystals like rose quartz, amethyst, and fluorite. It's also not recommended to leave very clear quartz crystal, such as the quartz in a crystal ball, in very bright or hot sunlight, as there is a slight risk of the concentrated heat igniting a fire.

A safe bet all around for all stones is moonlight. Again, outdoors is ideal, but a windowsill is also quite effective. Nights of the Full Moon are wonderfully magical times to clean, clear, and charge the stones, as the light of the Moon performs all three functions. Be sure to leave them for the entire night. You may even want to repeat the process for additional nights, depending on how the stones feel to you in the morning.

The element of Earth can be used either literally or figuratively by burying the stones in your yard for several days or in a bowl of soil, salt, or rice. Rice is gentler than salt, so use your best judgment according to the type of stone. Be sure to discard the rice or salt afterward, as it will have absorbed the unwanted energy; it often appears somewhat "dirty" after the clearing is over. If you're burying the stones outdoors, be sure to mark the spot so you'll be able to find them again. Many Witches recommend leaving them in the Earth for a full lunar cycle for extra powerful cleansing and charging.

To use the element of Air, you can burn sage or other purifying herbs and pass the stones through the smoke. Incense in a burner can do in a pinch, though it's better if you can use more traditional incense with charcoal and a fireproof dish, or a smudge bundle. Visualize the unwanted energy dissipating in the smoke, leaving the crystal clean, bright, renewed, and ready to be charged with your personal magical energy.

Cleaning and clearing your stones is not a one-time activity. You'll need to do this periodically. It's recommended, for example, to clear a stone that was used in a spell before using it in another, especially if the purposes of the spells are different. It's also important to note that crystals and stones do get dusty, such as when they sit in one place for long periods of time. If a stone is looking dull in color or if it's been in one place for so long that you don't even "see" it anymore when you scan the area, then it's time to give it some attention through cleaning and clearing.

Charging

For your magic to be effective, your tools should be charged before spellwork, whether you're working with a candle, a pentacle, or any other object. Crystals and stones are particularly fun to charge because they are essentially "batteries" that store and then release energy. Some Witches say that certain stones concentrate the personal energy you charge them with so that the power is even stronger when you use them in spellwork.

Spellwork isn't the only reason to charge your stones with your own positive energy. You may charge them for use in Wiccan rituals or for spiritual and emotional healing approaches that don't require a formal spell. For example, clean, clear, and charge a piece of bloodstone for increased physical strength, and it will boost its natural ability to help with this purpose. You might also charge a stone that you plan to use simply for enhancing your space, such as a large geode or piece of rose quartz.

As mentioned above, sunlight, moonlight, and the soil of the Earth are natural chargers for crystals and stones and can be handy as "one-step" methods for cleaning and charging. Other ways to charge your stones include laying them on a larger quartz or amethyst cluster, setting them near a chime or bell and then ringing it, and sprinkling them with flower petals or herbs. Rose petals and honeysuckle are particularly good for this, along with rosemary, sage, and thyme.

Many Witches like to match the charging method with the elemental energy of the stone. For example, the sun is great for stones with Fire energy, such as amber and garnet, while burying hematite or jasper in soil can amplify their Earth energies. Place amethyst or sodalite outdoors on a windy day to take advantage of their elemental resonance with Air. Charge some purified water, perhaps adding a pinch of a Water-linked herb like chamomile or thyme, then sprinkle it on moonstone or jade. Alternatively, you can match the charging method with your purpose for working with the stone. Soil is good for attracting Earth energies, such as strength and balance. Moonlight works well for psychic and spiritual enhancement. As you learn more about your stones, strengthen your intuition, and experiment with different methods, you'll learn which practices that serve you best.

For maximum effectiveness, it's best to charge crystals right after cleaning and clearing them when their energetic state is a blank slate, uninfluenced by the energy in the surrounding environment. However, when using a stone in spellwork, it's recommended to charge it specifically for the purpose you're working the spell for, even if you've previously charged it using one of the methods above (or one of your own devising). To do this, you can simply hold the stone in your dominant, or "power" hand, think about your goal, and visualize all of your magical energy flowing through your arm, into your hand, and into the stone. Hold this visualization until you feel intuitively that the stone is fully charged. Try to do this as close to the spellwork as possible for the strongest results.

Crystals in Your Daily Life

So, you've acquired a new crystal, and cleaned, cleared, and charged it. Now what? It's unlikely to just start working magic in your life without any effort on your part. To learn to use the energy of your new stone, you need to get acquainted with it. This can be accomplished through a variety of different practices. Start where your intuition tells you to, and don't be afraid to experiment. After a while, you'll develop your own ways of relating to your crystals and stones, and they will become a regular and beloved part of your daily life.

The simplest way of getting to know your crystal is to simply hold it in your hands, as you may have done when selecting it from the shop. Sit with it for a few minutes with your eyes closed, and just notice the sensations in your body and mind as they arise. See if you can feel whether the energy of the stone is projective or receptive. (Review the descriptions of these energies on pages 51–54.) If you have a regular meditation practice, incorporate crystals into it by either holding them or placing them near you as you meditate. Some stones, such as ametrine and just about any variety of quartz, are particularly well suited for meditation. These stones can help you clear your mind as you strengthen your connection with them. You can also place crystals under your pillow before going to sleep. Not all stones are ideal for this, but citrine, moonstone, and rose quartz can enhance the quality of your sleep as well as your dreams. Experiment and take note of the difference each type of stone makes.

Another easy way to develop a relationship with your crystals is to place them strategically in your living space. Many Witches keep crystals on their altars or elsewhere in their sacred space as well as throughout their home. You can find plenty of information on crystal placement using a feng shui approach: amethyst in the bedroom, for example, helps promote deep sleep, while jade placed near your front door attracts wealth. You can also simply place crystals in areas of your home that feel energetically "flat" or are otherwise in need of sprucing up. Try different stones in different places and feel out where they seem to "want" to be.

Some Witches prefer to keep their magical stones in a soft velvet or silk pouch, keeping them only for use in ritual and spellwork. This keeps the stones protected from exposure and any unwanted energy in their surrounding environment. However, if you can, try to leave your crystals in plain view, at least for a while after you've acquired them. Place several polished stones in a pretty bowl or even a clear glass jar. (If you go this route, leave the jar open rather than sealing their energy off with a lid.) Note that raw stones with rough edges or points can scratch polished stones, so avoid keeping the two types together in any container.

The more you see your crystals, the more you remember them, which helps you keep strengthening your connection with them. You may still wish to keep a select few stones put away for spellwork only, but if you have none in your immediate environment, it can be easy to forget that you have any at all, which can lead to missed opportunities to enhance your life.

Finally, wear and carry your crystals as much as possible. Many crystal retailers sell wire pendants that you can place your favorite stone in, and many stones are available as jewelry. You can also keep crystals and stones in your pockets, your purse— anywhere that keeps them close to your body at all times. Again, be mindful of scratches. Many stones are softer than you might expect, so avoid carrying stones in the same pocket as your keys or other objects that can damage the surface. Cloth pouches are handy for this reason and are usually available where crystals and stones are sold.

BRINGING IT ALL TOGETHER

NOW THAT YOU'VE BROUGHT A CRYSTAL OR TWO (OR THREE, or four!) into your life, you're ready to try your hand at some spellwork. Part three will introduce you to a few different types of crystal magic from simple "charge and carry" spells to ritual baths, joining the power of crystals with magically charged candles and herbs. Remember also to spend some time with the stone(s) you plan to work with in your magic. The power of spellwork is much more effective when you have a strong connection to the tools you work with, and this is especially true when working with these natural gifts from the Earth. As you experiment with the magical workings on the next several pages, approach them with reverence for the living energies of crystals, and, just as importantly, have fun!

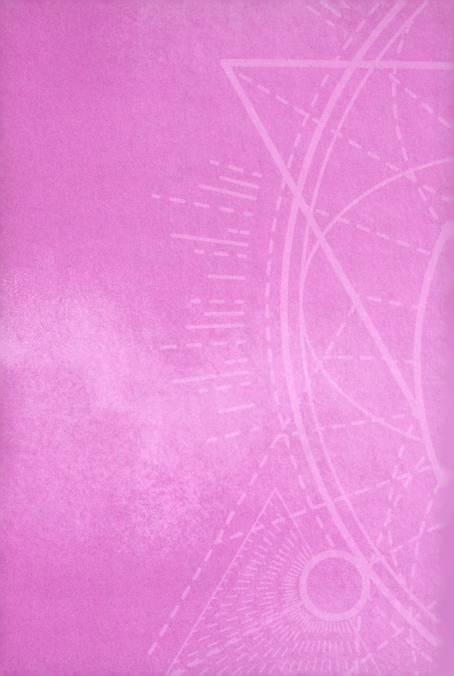

PART THREE

A CRYSTAL GRIMOIRE

PERSONALIZED STONE MAGIC

A GRIMOIRE IS A BOOK OF SPELLS, MAGICAL CORRESPON-
dences, and other esoteric information helpful to the practice of magic. Wiccans refer to their personal grimoire as a Book
of Shadows, which is traditionally kept secret, though plenty
of Witches like to share their spells and magical tips with one
another. The spellwork on the following pages is shared with the
intention of providing a jumping-off point into the many possibilities of crystal magic.

These spells focus exclusively on the thirteen stones profiled
on pages 32–50 to provide opportunities to deepen your acquain-
tance with them. However, as you set out to bring new crystals
into your life, always go with your intuition. If a stone outside of
the thirteen featured in this book calls to you, then by all means,
listen! Likewise, if you're looking for a particular stone for a spell,
like jade for example, but don't feel connected to any of the jade
stones you're seeing in the store, it may not be time for you to work
with jade or the jade for you may be elsewhere.

You can also make substitutions in many of the spells. It is often
the case that two or more alternative stones are equally suitable
to your magical purpose. This is especially good to remember if
you're on a budget that doesn't have room for another new crystal
just now. Remember, magic should never be a cause for financial
stress. Instead, it should be a means of creating more abundance!

When you find success with a spell you've tried, it's a good idea to record it in your own personal Book of Shadows or even just a notebook devoted to your magical practice. Include any alterations you may have made, and, of course, the results!

PREPARING FOR SUCCESSFUL SPELLWORK

THE INSTRUCTIONS FOR EACH SPELL IN THIS SECTION ASSUME that you have already cleaned, cleared, and charged your crystals for use in magic. Since many of the most effective methods for clearing and charging take a few to several hours, planning ahead will be important. Remember that charging is most effective right after clearing, and this process is best done as close to the actual spellwork as possible. However, this is not an absolute rule, so don't worry if you have to charge your stones a day or two ahead of time. Most of the spells below involve an additional charging process for the specific purpose of the work, which you can always do just before any spell.

It's equally important to prepare yourself mentally, emotionally, and spiritually for magic. Spells worked in a hurry without sufficient time to get in the right frame of mind are unlikely to be successful. Take time beforehand to clear your mind of any mundane distractions. Try meditating, taking a hot bath, doing some yoga, or any other way to wind down that you prefer. Likewise, avoid working spells when you are emotionally agitated—particularly if you are angry or upset. Take some deep breaths and wait until you've calmed down. If you're not mentally and emotionally clear, then you're not spiritually clear either, which will weaken the effect on your personal magical power. It can also lead to undesirable results!

For example, if you work a spell for increased abundance while you're feeling stressed about money, you might receive a promotion at your job that you don't actually want due to the extra pressure. That's why it's always best to add two "conditions" to any spellwork: with harm to none and for the good of all. Specifying your intention in this way ensures the best possible results. "Harm to none" means that no negative effects will befall anyone inadvertently as a result of the Universe realigning reality to meet your request (including you!). "For the good of all" ensures that what you're asking for is also in your best interest as well as the best interests of anyone else who may be involved in your situation.

It is ill-advised to perform spellwork that would attempt to harm or even manipulate another person. The three-fold law of

Witchcraft states than any work you do will come back to you three times over, so make sure you're working for positive results only! Even so-called "love spells" performed with a specific person in mind often tend to backfire, blocking rather than creating a connection between the spell caster and the object of desire. In fact, it's best to avoid working magic on another person's behalf without first obtaining permission.

If you're new to spellwork, you may find the noticeable effects from your efforts are subtle at best. This might just mean you're impatient to see results or that you're allowing doubt to cancel out the power of the work. Don't get discouraged—it takes time to learn how to truly connect with yourself as a power source and to focus that energy effectively as you send it out into the Universe. All practitioners of magic have to spend time developing and strengthening their skills. So, practice, persist, and don't be afraid to experiment with these and any other magical workings to see what works best for you.

CALLING A CRYSTAL INTO YOUR LIFE

If you've been unable to acquire any crystals or stones or if you're feeling that you'd like to bring more into your life, try asking the Universe directly to help you connect with the right stone(s) for you. This is an especially good spell to work prior to making online orders for crystals. Sea salt itself has a crystalline structure, which adds a magical boost to your intention.

☰ YOU WILL NEED ☰

1 white candle

Sea salt

☰ INSTRUCTIONS ☰

Sprinkle salt in a circle around the candle while saying the following (or similar) words:

"With this sacred salt of Earth, I ask the
perfect crystal to come into my life."

Close your eyes and visualize yourself surrounded by beautiful, sparkling crystals of every color. (Alternatively, if you're seeking a particular type of stone, make that the focus of your visualization.) Take a few deep breaths, then light the candle and say:

"It is so. Blessed Be."

SIMPLE CHARGE AND CARRY TALISMANS

ONE OF THE EASIEST AND MOST PORTABLE WAYS TO WORK crystal magic is to charge a small stone with a particular intention and then keep it with you in a pocket or locket as you go about your day. The energy of the crystal itself combines with the magical energy of your intention to reinforce the manifestation of your desire. In addition, your awareness of the charmed stone on your person helps remind you that the Universe is realigning itself to conform to your request. This type of spell is particularly useful for work concerning emotional, psychological, and/or spiritual challenges, such as boosting your courage when facing a daunting task or situation. However, you can also charge a stone for long-term goals, such as attracting prosperity or warding off sources of chronic negativity.

One reminder: if you carry stones in your pocket, be sure not to carry keys or any other sharp objects in the same pocket, as many of the stones used in magic can scratch easily. It's also best to avoid carrying polished and raw stones together, particularly raw crystal points, which can scratch the softer polished variety. As mentioned earlier, you can wrap polished stones in a soft cloth to avoid these risks, though some argue that this creates an unnecessary extra barrier between the stone's energy and your body. This may or may not be the case for you, however, so do what feels right for your circumstances. Finally, try to avoid carrying cell phones and other wireless devices with magically charged crystals, as it's possible that the emissions from these gadgets can interfere, however slightly, with the stone's energy field.

═ CREATING YOUR TALISMAN ═

This process can be used to charge any stone for any purpose, including the talismans for courage, balancing energy, and protection on pages 82–83. Try one or more of these examples, or create your own crystal talisman to suit your specific magical needs.

═ YOU WILL NEED ═

1 white, black, or purple candle (these are good colors for charging stones, but use a different color if you prefer)

1 or more amethyst and/or clear quartz crystal pieces (these crystals are excellent charge "boosters" but optional; if you don't have either crystal, you can still charge your talisman stone with your own energy)

1 stone to charge and carry (see individual talisman instructions on pages 82–83)

═ INSTRUCTIONS ═

Place the amethyst and/or quartz, if using, in front of the candle and light the wick. Hold your talisman stone in both hands. Close your eyes and take several deep breaths. Visualize yourself achieving the effect that you want the talisman to re-create later (see the individual instructions on pages 82–83 for examples). Using words of affirmation will help solidify the visualization, which is the expression of your intention for the talisman. When you sense that the stone has been programmed with the energy you're seeking to draw on later, place the stone near the amethyst/clear quartz and leave it with the candle burning for at least one hour. Then it's ready to take with you wherever you go, whenever you need it!

≡ A TALISMAN FOR COURAGE ≡

Crystal: carnelian
(can also use tiger's eye)

The perceived need for courage most often relates to specific situations, whether it's a job interview, a first date, or embarking on a new journey in life. As you hold the carnelian in your hands, visualize the circumstances that you need courage for. Now imagine yourself filled with bright orange light, radiating it outward like sunlight in all directions. Hold this light in your imagination as you see yourself triumphing in the situation. Say an affirmation out loud, such as:

"I stand in the fire of courage and walk bravely
into [name situation here]. So let it be."

≡ A TALISMAN FOR BALANCING ENERGY ≡

Crystal: jade
(can also use malachite)

Whether it's mood swings, exhaustion, restlessness, or all three at once, sometimes we just can't get into a good place physically and emotionally. For this visualization, hold the jade and imagine yourself filled with deep, soft, healing green light from head to toe. Don't think about any of the reasons for why you're feeling out of balance, as this will just reinforce the energy of distress. Simply focus on feeling calm and at peace. When you're ready to place the jade near the candle, say the following (or similar) words:

"I am balanced and healed from all disturbances. So let it be."

⚞ A TALISMAN FOR PROTECTION ⚟

Crystal: bloodstone
(can also use jet)

When energy imbalances are tied to a particular person or situation you encounter regularly, a protection stone can shield you from the negativity that may otherwise wreak havoc on your senses. Hold the bloodstone (or other stone with protective properties) and see yourself filled with and surrounded by white light. See how this light blinds and blocks any energy that is negative and unwelcome. Say the following (or similar) words:

"I am made of radiant white light, connected
to the core of Universal love."

Note: Because crystals used in protection usually absorb negative energy, it's a good idea to clear and recharge them more often than you might with those used in, say, a love or prosperity spell. Some stones absorb negativity at a faster rate than others, and some people and situations are more powerfully negative than others, so there's no hard and fast rule about when and how often to clear your stones, but pay attention to any you use for protection, and you'll start to get a feel for when it's time to do so.

CRYSTAL ELIXIRS

CRYSTAL ELIXIRS, SOMETIMES REFERRED TO AS "ESSENCES," are made by infusing water with the vibrations of a particular crystal or stone. They are used for physical, emotional, and spiritual healing as well as magic. The most common way of using them is by drinking the water, but they can also be used topically on the skin or added to bathwater. These simple, magical potions work through the body's direct absorption of the vibrations of the crystal, creating an alignment between your own energy and that of the stone chosen for the particular purpose.

An important warning: not all crystals are suitable for elixirs. In fact, many crystals and stones are highly toxic and should *never* be used in elixirs. Amazonite, azurite, cinnabar, emerald, lapis lazuli, malachite, and pyrite are just a few examples of minerals containing toxins that can leach into the water. And toxic crystals or minerals might be mixed in with the main elements in some stones, although they may not be immediately visible. There are also some stones that will even begin to dissolve in water, such as selenite and kunzite. (As a general rule, stones with names ending in "ite" are problematic when they come into contact with water.) If you are considering substitutions for the elixir spells following or branching out to create your own, this is not the time to simply "go with your gut." It is *very* important to do thorough research on any stone you're considering for use in an elixir. It's also recommended to use polished stones rather than raw, since there is even less likelihood of any unwanted mineral traces leaching into the water.

For any stones you're uncertain about, you can always charge the water indirectly by placing the stone in a smaller jar within a larger bowl or jar of water.

SIMPLE ELIXIRS

The instructions below are for creating a simple elixir to be used within a day or two. For longer-lasting elixirs, you'll need to use a preservative—usually brandy, vodka, or distilled vinegar. The advantage of taking this extra step is that you can use the elixir multiple times over an extended period of time—just a few drops will usually suit most purposes. For the sake of keeping it simple, this step is not included below, but it can be easily researched online if you want to take your work with elixirs to the next level.

YOU WILL NEED

Clear glass bowl (a drinking glass is an appropriate substitute)

1 crystal or stone of your choice

Spring water or purified water (tap water will do in a pinch, but it's best to at least filter it, if possible)

Clear lid or plastic wrap (optional)

3 to 5 quartz crystals (optional)

INSTRUCTIONS

Place the cleared and charged stone in the bowl, focusing on your magical intention for the elixir. Slowly pour the water over the stone, using at least enough water to make one glass but not much more. Next, allow the crystal's vibrations to charge the water. This can take from just a couple of hours to overnight, depending on how you choose to do it. Many Witches like to use sunlight, leaving the elixir in the windowsill or even outside, in full sun, for 2 to 4 hours. This method doesn't work on cloudy days, however, and isn't recommended for stones that fade in sunlight, such as colored quartzes and fluorite. Moonlight is a good alternative, provided that some amount of moonlight shines directly on the water for at least 2 hours. If you use moonlight, leave the elixir out overnight and retrieve it before dawn. Cover outdoor elixirs with a clear lid or plastic wrap to keep out bugs. In addition, you can place 3 to 5 quartz crystals around the elixir to strengthen the vibrational quality of the water, but this is entirely up to you.

It's also possible to simply leave the elixir indoors overnight, either covered or in the refrigerator. The stone will release its vibrations into the water whether or not sunlight or moonlight are involved—it's just nice to have the added enhancement of natural light. So, if neither sunlight nor moonlight is a possibility for you, don't let that stop you. And if you can use quartz crystals around the elixir, as mentioned above, this can definitely raise the quality of the charged water.

Once the elixir is charged, pour the water into a drinking glass or a jar—preferably not made of plastic or metal—and catch the stone in your hand before it tumbles out into the new container. Thank the stone for its energy and its presence in your life. Your elixir will be good for 24 hours or so.

CITRINE EMPOWERMENT ELIXIR

With its capacity to energize and increase motivation, citrine makes for an excellent elixir to boost self-confidence and will-power. Try this spell particularly if you're struggling with sluggishness, procrastination, or anxiety about work or school or if you've been feeling as if you're in a rut in your overall life. As you place the citrine and pour the water, visualize how you will feel when your particular challenge has been overcome and welcome a feeling of excitement about the future. Because citrine is strongly associated with the Sun, this elixir is best when charged outdoors, but if this isn't possible, you can place it under bright light (not too near the lightbulb) or near a lit candle next for a few hours.

As you prepare to drink the elixir, take a deep breath, calm your mind, and state the outcome you wish to manifest. You might say, for example:

"I now activate my power to triumph over this challenge and stand in confidence about the future."

Then take a drink and thank the citrine for its empowering energies. You may wish to continue sipping the full elixir over the next few hours, sprinkle some on your skin, or add it to bathwater. However, you choose to use it, be present and remember your goal each time you interact with the charged water.

SPIRITUAL ENERGY AMETHYST ELIXIR

When the hectic details of everyday life are causing you to feel disconnected from the spiritual and psychic realms, this elixir helps raise your vibration above the mundane level and get back on track with your higher self. For best results, try charging this elixir with moonlight, and/or place pieces of moonstone around the water while charging. When you're ready to drink the elixir, center and ground yourself, holding the glass with both hands. Take a few deep breaths and speak your intention to the Universe. For example, you might say:

> *"Thank you, spirit of amethyst, for opening my path to communication with Divine Self. I am ready to receive any guidance waiting for me on the higher plane."*

Take a sip and then spend several minutes in meditation, continuing to hold the elixir in both hands. You will eventually feel at peace, released from mental clutter and able to tap into your authentic inner wisdom.

CRYSTAL BATH SPELLS

USING CRYSTALS IN THE BATH IS A GREAT WAY TO CREATE AN energy adjustment for the body, mind, and soul. Similar to the way elixirs work, the vibrations of the crystals infuse the water with their balancing energies. Clear quartz and rose quartz are safe popular crystals to use in this way. If you're wishing to experiment with other crystals and stones, remember to research them first, as some stones will dissolve in water and may be toxic to the skin. Also, be sure to rinse and recharge stones after using them in the bath.

QUARTZ CRYSTAL CLARITY BATH

Clear quartz is a wonderful stone to work with when you're facing a tough decision or confusing situation. Its energies promote the dispelling of illusion caused by conscious and unconscious emotional attachments. Feel free to repeat this ritual bath as often as you wish, as it can work wonders for dilemmas both large and small.

YOU WILL NEED

1 or more clear quartz crystals

Several small amethysts (optional)

¼ cup (55 g) sea salt

1 white candle

Run the bath until the tub is at least halfway full. Place the clear quartz crystal(s) in the water, asking for guidance regarding your situation as you do so. Place the amethysts, if using, around the edges of the tub. Add the sea salt under the running water. When the bath is ready, light the white candle, turn off any artificial lighting in the bathroom, and climb in. Stay in the bath for at least 20 minutes and allow your mind and body to relax. Don't worry if you don't come up with an answer or solution while you're in the water! You may need to "sleep on it" for a night or more before the resolution to your issue makes itself apparent.

LOVE AND HARMONY BATH

Rose quartz both attracts and promotes love of all kinds, whether it involves close friendship, romance, or family relationships. Try this ritual bath whenever you feel the need for a boost of positive, loving vibrations in your life. If you're looking to attract a romantic partner or improve an existing romantic relationship, you may wish to use a red candle, but pink will do the trick in all situations involving love. The lavender oil helps dissipate anxiety and negative emotions, clearing the way for more harmonic energy in your life.

YOU WILL NEED

1 or more rose quartz crystals

3 to 5 drops lavender essential oil

1 pink or red candle

INSTRUCTIONS

Run the bath until the tub is at least halfway full. Place the rose quartz in the water, visualizing the result you desire, whether it's improved communication between yourself and a friend or family member or a healthy, loving romantic relationship. When the bath is full, add the lavender essential oil to the water. Light the candle, turn off any artificial lighting in the bathroom, and climb in. Conjure up the feeling you want to have in your heart when your desired result is manifested. Stay in the bath for at least 20 minutes. If you can, remain in the tub while draining the water, as the energy of the rose quartz tends to have a stronger effect that way.

CRYSTAL AND CANDLE SPELLS

CRYSTALS AND CANDLES MAKE GREAT PARTNERS IN MAGIC, symbolizing the elements of Earth and Fire. This type of crystal magic also allows for more flexibility when it comes to creating your own variations, as you can use any kind of stone you like without worrying about toxicity or water damage. Here are three simple spells to start off with. You can use votive candles or tea lights, but spell candles are ideal, as they burn all the way down in a few hours or less. Be sure to charge your candles beforehand as well as your crystals with your personal magical energy. And remember that you should never leave a burning candle unattended!

CITRINE PROSPERITY SPELL

Citrine is an ideal stone for prosperity work, as its bright, sunny energy helps you retain the optimism needed to make room for new wealth in your life. After working this spell, place the crystals somewhere prominent in your home or office for a week or so, to remind you of the positive intention you've sent out into the Universe.

=== YOU WILL NEED ===

4 citrine crystals

1 green candle

Arrange the crystals in a circle around the candle. Touch each one with your power hand and directly charge it for the purposes of prosperity. You might say something like "I now charge this crystal with the power to connect with the source of infinite wealth." After charging each crystal, close your eyes and visualize how you will feel when there are no money concerns to trouble you, all your bills are paid, and you have plenty left over to enjoy life with. When you have a strong sense of this feeling, light the candle and say the following (or similar) words:

"I manifest prosperity in my daily life,
having all that I need and more."

Leave the crystals in place until the candle burns out on its own.

CONFLICT RESOLUTION SPELL

At the heart of any conflict is a need to communicate clearly, honestly, and with compassion. In this spell, each person involved in the conflict is represented by a lapis lazuli stone, the stone of truth, communication, and connection to higher self. Because you have at least one other person in mind when working this spell, you must be careful to remain positive, or at the very least, neutral, in your thoughts about them. Don't mistake the spell as one that gives you control over another's thoughts or behavior. Instead, focus on the peaceful outcome of having your conflict resolved.

**2 or more lapis lazuli stones, one for each person
involved in the situation**

1 blue candle

≡ INSTRUCTIONS ≡

Take a few moments to ground and center yourself. Hold each lapis stone individually in your hands for a minute and visualize yourself letting go of any feelings you may be harboring about the conflict. When you feel ready, place the stones on either side of the candle (make a circle if using more than two). As you place each stone, say:

"May peace, light, and truth radiate from this gift of the Earth."

Light the candle and say the following (or similar) words:

*"This conflict is now resolved, for the good
of all and harm to none. So let it be."*

Allow the candle to burn out on its own. You may wish to carry one of the stones in your pocket for a while, especially the next time you interact with the person(s) involved in the conflict.

SPELL FOR BLESSING A NEW HOME

Amethyst is a wonderful feel-good crystal when it comes to creating a positively charged atmosphere in the home. While this spell is particularly good for blessing a place you've just moved into, it can also be used to create a new sacred space within your home, no matter how long you've lived in it. You can even try it after remodeling or significantly rearranging the furniture in your home to put the finishing energetic touches on the renewal you've manifested.

YOU WILL NEED

Lemon or myrrh essential oil (optional)

1 or more amethyst quartz crystals

1 white candle

INSTRUCTIONS

If using essential oil, place a drop on each piece of amethyst. Then place the crystal(s) next to the candle. Visualize white light suffusing the entirety of your house (or the space within your house that you're designating as sacred space). Say words of affirmation, such as:

"This space is a blessing point of sacred energy. Within these walls are happiness, prosperity, and well-being. So let it be."

Light the candle and allow it to burn out on its own. Keep the amethyst(s) somewhere prominent in your home or sacred space, as they will continue to emit positive vibrations.

BURIED CRYSTAL SPELLS

THESE SPELLS DIRECTLY USE THE POWER OF EARTH BY returning the crystals to their source. Raw stones are ideal for this type of magical work, as their natural surfaces have not been ground away in the tumbling process, but polished stones are also perfectly fine to use. The strength of your focused intention is more important than whether the crystal is raw or polished.

A CRYSTAL MONEY SPELL

When you have a specific need and aren't sure how it will be met, this spell can be quite successful. Whether you're facing a costly repair to your car or an unexpected shortfall that jeopardizes your ability to cover the bills, draw on the power of your favorite money-attracting stone for help. Don't forget to mark the place where you bury the stone so that you can find it again!

YOU WILL NEED

1 green candle

Pencil and small piece of paper

1 carnelian, jade, or other prosperity stone of your choice

INSTRUCTIONS

Light the candle and then write your name and your need on the piece of paper, both the amount of money needed and the purpose.

(For example, "$500.00 for the car repair.") Don't write "I need," as you're working to transform from a place of need into a place of *having*. Fold it several times, and set the stone on top of it, saying the following (or similar) words:

"Universe, thank you for all you provide. With this [name the stone], I call the solution to my need into my life."

Leave the stone on top of the paper until the candle burns out. Bury the stone and paper in your yard. (If this is not possible, a potted plant will work.) Leave it until your money need is met. Once it is, be sure to unearth the crystal and paper and give thanks to the Universe! Doing so will help you increase your magical power for future spellwork.

BAD HABIT BANISHING SPELL

While the main work of getting rid of an unwanted habit is up to you, magic can certainly create a very helpful boost of willpower and favorable circumstances. Bloodstone and jet are two excellent choices for this banishing spell, but always work with your instincts and your relationship with your crystals. You won't be retrieving this one, so make sure to use a stone you can part with!

≡ YOU WILL NEED ≡

1 black candle

Pencil and small piece of paper

Bloodstone, jet, or other banishing stone of your choice

Light the candle and then write the habit you want to break on the piece of paper. Hold the stone in your palms and spend several minutes visualizing your life without this habit—how you will feel on a daily basis and the benefits you will receive. Conjure up a

feeling of freedom, relief, and joy. Then tear the paper up into small pieces, gather them into a pile, and set the stone on top of the pile until the candle burns down.

Take the stone to a location far from your home—preferably somewhere you rarely, if ever, find yourself in. This could be a park across town, or, ideally, a wooded or otherwise rural location. Bury the stone in the Earth. When you're finished, brush the dirt from your hands vigorously over the spot where the stone is buried and say the following (or similar) words:

"I now release the habit of [name the habit] to the past, where it will always remain."

Then walk away without looking back.

MAGICAL CREATIONS

CRYSTALS CAN BE THOUGHT OF AS PERFECT SYMBOLS OF THE creative energies of the Universe, as they are the direct results of the Earth's own creative processes. As such, these stones can be great additions to magical crafts, such as Witch bottles, honey jars, charm bags, and homemade wands. The following examples are simple for beginners, easy on the budget, and adaptable to different purposes—just use herbs, stones, and spell words appropriate to your magical goal.

A GROUNDING AND CENTERING JAR

After a busy day, it can seem hard to take the time to ground and center enough to perform successful spellwork. Many a Witch has put off spellwork that would be beneficial simply because getting in the right frame of mind seems like so much work!

This spellcraft can become something of a shortcut, helping you get to a place of calm and quiet more quickly. Try meditating with it in your hands for a few moments before preparing for magical work or anytime you just need a "time out" during your day. Of course, you must be well grounded and centered when creating and blessing the jar for it to continue to give that grounding energy back to you!

1 tablespoon dried sage

1 tablespoon dried lavender flowers

1 tablespoon dried sandalwood or patchouli

Mortar and pestle (if you don't have one, you can use a
bowl and spoon)

1 clear glass empty spice jar (or another small jar) with lid

3 pieces hematite

≡ **INSTRUCTIONS** ≡

Place each herb in the mortar and pestle, affirming with each that
its purpose is to ground and center you. You can say something
like the following:

> *"Sage, thank you for grounding and centering
> me from within this jar. Blessed Be"*

Do the same with the lavender and the sandalwood or patchouli.
Gently mix the herbs together and pour them into the jar. Then,
sit and hold the hematite in the palms of your hands and spend
several minutes deepening your sense of being grounded and centered. Place them gently in the jar and close the lid. Hold the jar in
your hands and say the following (or similar) words:

> *"From now on, this jar returns me to the
> Earth and to my center. Blessed Be."*

You may wish to keep the jar on your altar or in your sacred
space. For extra help with grounding and centering, remove the lid
from time to time and inhale the scent of the herbs.

MOONSTONE CHARM FOR PSYCHIC RECEPTIVITY

Many of us experience periods of heightened intuition, when we just seem to ride along on a current of subtle impulses and messages that lead us to make fortuitous choices and find solutions to problems. But living in a fast-paced world means that we can lose that flow fairly often and may struggle to tune back into our innate connection with Universal energy. This spell helps you open your psychic receptivity more consistently so that you can stay in that flow for longer stretches of time. Stay committed to the practice of connecting with your moonstone for at least seven days, and you'll notice a difference in how you respond to the day-to-day moments of your life, as your inner voice guides you along your path.

A silk or muslin drawstring bag is ideal so that you can see the stones and herbs through the bag.

≡ YOU WILL NEED ≡

1 white candle

1 medium sized moonstone

Pentacle slab or small plate

Small see-through drawstring bag

1 tablespoon dried mugwort and/or dandelion leaf

Journal or writing paper (optional)

Light the candle and hold the moonstone between your palms for a few moments. Close your eyes and take three deep breaths, focusing only on your inhale and exhale. When your mind is clear, simply focus on the energy of the stone and take note of any physical sensations or psychic impressions you may experience. Don't worry if you don't notice or feel anything significant; you're just attuning to the stone and practicing being in the present moment.

When you're ready, place the moonstone on the pentacle slab or plate. Sprinkle the herbs in a circle around the stone, while saying the following (or similar) words:

"Light of the Moon,
power of stone,
I open myself to what can be known,
and learn how to listen."

Set the slab or plate out under direct moonlight, either outdoors or on a windowsill, and leave it there overnight. The candle can be left burning or gently extinguished and used for atmosphere another time.

In the morning, place the moonstone in the drawstring bag and add the herbs. Keep the charm on your person or very close to you consistently for seven days. Keep it in your pocket or attach the bag to a cord to wear around your neck. Place it under your pillow just before bed to invite psychic messages into your dreams. (Some people find this too intense, so alternatively you can keep it on your nightstand, as close to your head as possible.) You can take the moonstone out of the bag to hold in your hand if you like, which is an especially excellent thing to do while meditating. Otherwise, leave the stone in with the herbs.

Throughout the seven days, be sure to write down any impressions, visions, or other types of messages you get. At the end of the week, do some freewriting about your overall experience with the spell. What have your dreams been like? Have you been noticing more synchronicities? Have you had an easier time making small decisions by listening to your gut? Finally, write about any current questions or issues you would like help with, and trust that you'll begin to receive answers from the Universe. Keep your moonstone charm where you can see it often or continue to keep it with you!

CONCLUSION

⎯⎯⎯⎯

CRYSTALS ARE SUCH MARVELOUS MAGICAL BEINGS. YOU CAN have a crystal in your life for decades and still see something new in it every time you pick it up, turning it at various angles and in different types of light. It is truly a gift to be able to tap into the energies of these stones—to the energy source of Earth in its many different expressions. Hopefully, this book has given you a starting place for your own explorations into the world of crystals and mineral stones and a desire to forge your own path.

The spells, rituals, and recipes in this beginner's guide represent just a handful of the infinite possibilities for crystal magic. As you grow in your practice, you will no doubt discover more types of magical workings, new methods and approaches to magic, and a stronger sense of what works best for you. You might try making personalized tweaks to the spells offered here, and you might even eventually create your own spells! Whatever the case, be sure to continue reading widely about crystals (and any other form of magic that interests you), as gathering diverse perspectives from multiple practitioners helps you hone your own intuition. To that end, a list of suggested resources is provided on pages 111–12.

It's also important to listen to your crystals and stones, as they will often seek to guide you on your path to spiritual wisdom and magical success. When you feel a certain stone tugging at you for your attention, pick it up, hold it for a while, and look up its magical associations and healing qualities. What is the stone offering to help you with right now? Or, possibly more to the point, what is the stone telling you about how it can help right now? The more you allow your crystals to communicate with you and take any recommended action based on their messages, the clearer your connection with them will become.

Never forget that crystals are living creations from deep inside the Earth, so always respect their energy and power, and take good care of them. Continue to hold them, meditate with them, make magic with them, and treasure them for as long as they remain with you.

CRYSTALS AND STONES
TABLE OF CORRESPONDENCE

CRYSTAL	COLOR(S)	MAGICAL USES
AMETHYST	Violet	Sharpens mental focus and intuition, clears sacred space
BLOODSTONE	Green with flecks of red/gold	Promotes physical healing, fertility, and abundance
CARNELIAN	Red/orange	Wards off negative energies, inspires courage
CITRINE	Yellow	Aids self-confidence, renewal, and useful dreams
HEMATITE	Silver/gray/shiny black	Strengthens willpower and confidence, helps with problem-solving
JADE	Green with flecks of red/gold	Promotes emotional balance, harmony, and wisdom; protects from negativity

CRYSTAL	COLOR(S)	MAGICAL USES
JET	Black	Supports transitions through grounding and centering, protection from negativity
LAPIS LAZULI	Blue/dark blue	Helps with altered consciousness, meditation, divination
MALACHITE	Green with bands of dark green and black	Supports spiritual growth and emotional courage, helpful during big change
MOONSTONE	White/pale blue	Supports intuition and wisdom, psychic receptivity, creativity
QUARTZ CRYSTAL	White/clear	Promotes healing, clarity, spiritual development
ROSE QUARTZ	Pink	Promotes emotional healing, love, and friendship
TIGER'S EYE	Brown/tan/gold with bands of black	Provides protection and energy

ACKNOWLEDGMENTS

MY DEEPEST THANKS TO MY FAMILY AND FRIENDS FOR UNCON-ditional love and support. To Audrey, for so many things, but in this particular case for the night the Tarot reading cracked the quartz. To Mina, who always gets it. And of course, to the stones themselves for their quiet and gentle wisdom.

To Barbara Berger at Sterling, for making this new edition of *Wicca Crystal Magic* a reality, and to Elysia Liang for her thoughtful edits. To Elizabeth Lindy for the beautiful cover design; Gina Bonanno and Sharon Jacobs for the stunning interior design conception, direction, and layout; Linda Liang for image research; production editor Michael Cea; and production manager Ellen Day-Hudson.

THANKS TO THE NEW AGE MOVEMENT, THERE'S BEEN NO shortage of books available on crystals and their use in physical, emotional, and spiritual healing, but the twenty-first century has also seen a proliferation of books on the use of crystals in magic. This brief list covers just a few of the most popular titles from the past two decades. Most are focused on crystal magic within Wiccan and other Witchcraft traditions, while a couple offer expanded information on the physical, emotional, and spiritual healing properties of mineral stones.

As with any other magic-related topic, however, be wary of accepting any one source as an ultimate authority. This is especially crucial when it comes to using potentially toxic crystals! Read widely, use your best judgment and enjoy learning more about the incredible power that crystals and stones have to offer.

Armády, Naha. *Everyday Crystal Rituals: Healing Practices for Love, Wealth, Career, and Home*. Emeryville, CA: Althea Press, 2018.

Conway, D.J. *Crystal Enchantments: A Complete Guide to Stones and Their Magical Properties*. New York: Crossing Press, 1999.

Cunningham, Scott. *Cunningham's Encyclopedia of Crystal, Gem & Metal Magic*. St. Paul, MN: Llewellyn, 2002.

Fogg, Kiera. *Crystal Gridwork: The Power of Crystals and Sacred Geometry to Heal, Protect, and Inspire.* Newbury Port, MA: Quarto Publishing, 2018.

Grant, Ember. *The Book of Crystal Spells: Magical Uses for Stones, Crystals, Minerals . . . and Even Sand.* Woodbury, MN: Llewellyn, 2013, 2019.

Greenleaf, Cerridwen. *The Magic of Crystals & Gems: Unlocking the Supernatural Power of Stones.* Miami: Mango, 2017.

Hall, Judy. *101 Power Crystals: The Ultimate Guide to Magical Crystals, Gems, and Stones for Healing and Transformation.* Beverly, MA: Fair Winds Press, 2011.

———. *The Crystal Bible: A Definitive Guide to Crystals.* Hampshire, UK: Godsfield Press, 2003.

Kynes, Sandra. *365 Days of Crystal Magic: Simple Practices with Gemstones and Minerals.* Woodbury, MN: Llewellyn, 2018.

———. *Crystal Magic: Mineral Wisdom for Pagans & Wiccans.* Woodbury, MN: Llewellyn, 2017.

PICTURE CREDITS

Alamy: Fisherman: 74

ClipArt.com: 90

Depositphotos.com: ©Katja87: 122; ©NadezhdaSh: throughout (radiating crescent eye, rays, lotus pendants), 115 (dreamcatcher), 121 (sun star)

Getty Images: *DigitalVision Vectors:* bauhaus1000: 58, 98; GeorgePeters: 83; Man_Half-tube: 97; Nastasic: 56; powerofforever: 2; ZU_09: 30, 77; *iStock/Getty Images Plus:* geraria: 100; kotoffei: throughout (stars); mart_m: 50, 94 (planets); Nadezhda_Shuparskaia: iii (hexagram sun); xii, 5, 8, 22, 26, 54, 60, 61, 78, 103, 120, 121 (ender); olegagafonov: iv, vii; Pimpay: 93, 103 (sac het); PinkPueblo: 61; polygraphus: 34 (sun face); Ksenija Purpisa: iv, v, vi, vii (sun in circle with arrow); ix, 6, 9, 11, 23, 96 (earth moon cycle); xi, 4,7,10, 18, 37, 43, 80, 90, 93, 94, 95, 97, 100 (radiating moon evolution); 51, 63, 90, 92, 100 (hanging crystal); 71, 86 (radiating pentagram); 95 (house); 103, 113 (crescent moon face); tschitscherin: i, 121 (pentagram); vectortatu: 56, 81, 82, 83, 91, 106, 107 (arrows); Vladayoung: 18 (crystal ball), 109

Internet Archive: 15

Rijksmuseum: 110

Shutterstock: Artur Balytskyi: 35, 36, 38, 41, 42, 44, 45, 46, 49 (zodiac); chempina: 79; Croisy: 105; Epine: 39, 103 (leaves); HikaruD88: 24; Alenka Karabanova: 10; MoreVector: 86; Morphart Creation: x; mountain beetle: 52; nadilia_oborska: 71; Mila Okie: 66, 120; Peratek: 69; Nadezhda Shuparskaia: ix, 6, 9, 11, 23, 27, 51, 55, 63, 76, 78, 79, 84, 87, 88, 89, 92, 96, 99, 101, 108 (lotus pendant); xiii, 108, 122 (lotus moon); Alena Solonshchikova: 33, 34, 37, 38, 40, 41, 43, 44, 46, 47, 48, 50, 80, 103 (stones); Bodor Tivadar: 7; VeraPetruk: 4; Vlada Young: 48; Katya Zlobina: 35

Wellcome Collection: 19

Courtesy of Wikimedia Commons: 13

INDEX

ABOUT THE AUTHOR

LISA CHAMBERLAIN is the successful author of more than twenty books on Wicca, divination, and magical living, including *Wicca Book of Spells*, *Wicca for Beginners*, *Runes for Beginners*, and *Magic and the Law of Attraction*. As an intuitive empath, she has been exploring Wicca, magic, and other esoteric traditions since her teenage years. Her spiritual journey has included a traditional solitary Wiccan practice as well as more eclectic studies across a wide range of belief systems. Lisa's focus is on positive magic that promotes self-empowerment for the good of the whole.

You can find out more about her and her work at her website, wiccaliving.com.

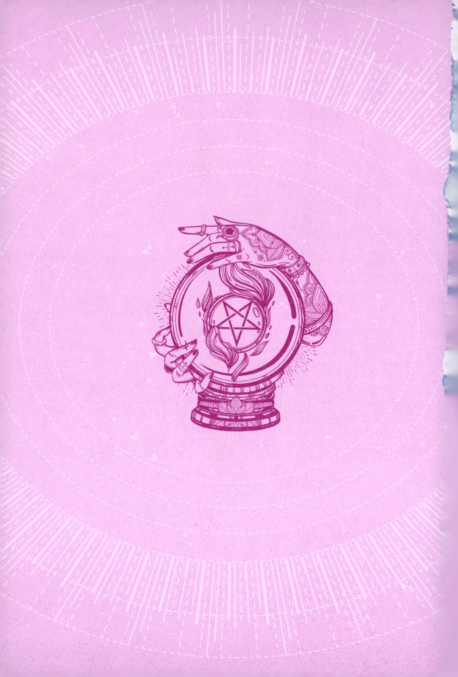